Eyes Wide Open

Charleston, SC
www.PalmettoPublishing.com

Eyes Wide Open
Copyright © 2023 by Milt Rodriguez

Paperback ISBN: 979-8-8875-7950-4
eBook ISBN: 979-8-8229-1574-9

Eyes Wide Open

Open

Seeing the Unseen

MILT RODRIGUEZ

CREDITS

Cover Art

The Woman (the Church) seeing with *eyes wide open*. Though she is in the heavenlies, she has her focus on the earth. She is in the heavenlies to know Him and yet on the earth to express Him.

Thanks to Derek Batty for this wonderful cover art.

Editing

Thanks to Alison Hardy for her incredibly detailed work in editing my very rough writings.

Encouragement

Thanks to my more than wonderful (and beautiful) wife Shari for encouragement and putting up with me during the process!

FORWARD BY JON ZENS

This is a beautiful, much-needed book! I am elated that a work like this is finally available to the Body of Christ. Milt shows how everything flows from the Lord's eternal purpose in Christ, and His heart to have a Bride express the Son on earth. I encourage you to get this book into the hands of new and young believers, so that they can know the Lord in deeper ways, and avoid the pitfalls associated with "going to church." This book will also be a balm for seasoned believers who have come to realize that following Christ must be more than programs and pews.

The author reminds us that the Father has put His seal (signet) on His Son. When He gives us anything, He gives us Jesus. So much religious busy-ness is focused on matters that in reality distract us from Christ. Milt asks:

Are you blinded by the end times, speaking in tongues, spiritual gifts, studying and memorizing the Bible, prayer, evangelism, social action, spiritual warfare, discipleship, authoritarianism, going to church on Sunday, pastoral leadership, or any of the other seemingly endless barrage of Christian teachings and practices?

Our Life in Christ is not about numerous issues that so easily catch our eye, but about the Life in the Vine coming to expression in the branches, both individually and as a Body.

One of the key components of the New Covenant is, "No longer will a person teach his neighbor, saying, 'Know the Lord,' because they will all know Me from the least to the greatest." "Know" is a special relational word, like a man "knowing" a woman. *Eyes Wide Open* will help people "know the Lord" in deeper, untold ways!

-- Jon Zens, author of *We Are Christ On Earth* and
Elusive Community

INTRODUCTION

Eyes Wide Open is an attempt at compiling all of my own knowledge and experiences in knowing Jesus Christ in a deeply inward way. I will also be drawing from the reservoir of experiences from my co-workers and the churches we have planted, along with the testimonies and lives of other saints who have walked this way down through the ages.

This book is coming at a time in my life when I am taking a season of an extended break from most ministry. I have been planting "organic" churches full-time for the last nine years and training new (younger) workers to plant organic churches as I do. I have also been doing many conferences and retreats with individuals and churches and connecting with many brothers and sisters in and out of the institutional church to help them understand how they can know the Lord in a deeper way and can experience and express Him in a corporate way (as known as "the church").

So this time of rest is definitely needed!

I have sensed the leading of the Lord for a few years to write this book. However, I must honestly confess some hesitation about writing something like this. I have, for many years, strongly believed that this knowledge is better served to be explained and experienced from within the context of the local authentic body life of the church of Jesus Christ. That is the proper environment for this teaching and experience. The tendency (in our individualistic culture) is to take this kind of material and appropriate it individually but not corporately. This is a mistake because the Lord's goal in all that He does is to build the church and thus express His own life through her.

The Lord has been dealing with me about this attitude. Who am I to make this determination? What right do I have to withhold something from God's people that could significantly help them spiritually? How do I know that God won't use this book to actually help encourage groups of believers to get together and practice it, thus causing more fellowship and possible true community life in Christ? Oh, Milt, you silly, silly man! Actually "foolish" would be a better word for it.

When I was in my early twenties, I began a search to know the Lord deeply in a very internal way. I was not happy having a lukewarm, anemic fellowship with the Lord. I wanted intimacy. I wanted to know Him deeply and completely. I wasn't satisfied settling for an outward, works-based relationship with Him. I wasn't satisfied knowing Him only by the typical "Christian" ways of knowing Him such as Bible study, prayer, "going to church," tithing, witnessing, and giving to missions. There had to be something more—I just knew it! And there must have been others who experienced this wonderful fellowship in the past and in the present whom I could learn from. There just had to be! And I was going to find them and learn from them.

During this time, I got a hold of a book by a woman named Jeanne Guyon who lived in France during the sixteen-hundreds. It was called *A Short and Easy Method of Prayer*. (I would definitely recommend you read Jeanne Guyon's books. Just keep in mind that she was Roman Catholic and really had no insight into the church. I have read many books by the so-called Catholic mystics and have included some in the list of recommended reading at the end of this book.) I can say without hesitation that her book changed my life forever!

Guyon's book was just the beginning. I started practicing her methods as shared in that book and others. It was revolutionary. I began to see the Lord in everything and everywhere. And probably most importantly, I began to see Him inside of me and inside my brothers and sisters! Wow! What a revolutionary vision. I then read a book by Brother Lawrence called *The Practice of the Presence of God*. This book greatly helped me learn to practice the very presence of God in every situation. At any rate, it just grew from there. However, there was a problem: I didn't know any other believers who knew or practiced such things.

Whenever I shared what I was learning with others I got that famous "thousand-yard stare." People thought that I was either crazy, possessed, or into some kind of weird new-age thing. In fact, I still get that sometimes. This brings up a good point for you, my dear reader.

At first, some of these things may seem so foreign to you that you will also think perhaps I have lost my mind. I assure you that I have not (despite what my wife says!). Just kidding. Hopefully, as you read this book, many lights will go on, so to speak. No doubt, you will find yourself asking why you have never heard these things before. But you need to be fair-warned that these things are not widely shared within the confines of traditional Christianity. (The reason for this would take a whole other book to explain. As early as the second century, things started going downhill in a hurry.)

The book is broken down into three parts:

Part One covers the spiritual and scriptural foundation for knowing the Lord. It will begin with the spiritual revelation of Christ. Who is this Christ in whom we are to place all of our trust?

Part Two covers spiritual and practical ways to know this Christ as an individual. What are our filters? How can we see Christ in all things? What does it mean to behold the Lord?

Part Three covers the spiritual and practical ways to know the Lord as the church. How do we express Him in the earth? How does the church function as the body? How does the church live as a family and community with Christ as the center and head? How do we, as the branches, abide in the vine?

There is something that I maintain very strongly and will repeatedly share throughout this book: the eternal purpose of God. In a nutshell, that purpose is that the living triune God desires to have an image (or an expression) of His character, power, and Person in a corporate community or body of humans. That is the reason that He created us and, in fact, the reason He created anything to begin with! This means that our relationship with Him is not to be individual only. His goal and purpose is to have a family, a house, a city of humans who are living by His divine life in this realm, for all realms (visible and invisible) to see.

I will also be using practical exercises or applications throughout the book. The apostle Paul always started his letters with the spiritual; that is, Christ Himself. Then, he would move toward the practical. So, I will take this format. Therefore, the end of each chapter will include practical exercises and applications. In these exercises, I will ask you to practice the ways of fellowshipping with the Lord that I have just shared. It's not enough to simply teach and preach Jesus Christ, as glorious as that is. We also need to show other believers how to practically know this Christ and live by the indwelling life of this Christ.

I strongly recommend that you follow through with these exercises since it will make the spiritual realities shared practical, and therefore, obtainable for you. Some of these exercises will require you to meet with another believer, or two, or three.

So, there you have it. I am unleashing upon the world spiritual realities and revelation that I received from our abundantly gracious Lord over the last forty years plus. Many of these things I received from others and I am forever grateful to those saints.

Brothers and sisters, we need to know the Lord. We need to know Him intimately and we need to know Him deeply. And, for His sake, we need to know Him together!

PROLOGUE

Before I dive into this book, I wanted to share something with you that you may not have ever consid-ered. It's something I have pon-dered for quite some time now (years) and I believe that I have some-what of an answer, though the depths of it are unending. Therefore, none of us has the whole picture alone. It's only as we come together as the Lord's body that we will see the completed picture.

It is an indisputable fact that at no other time in history has the church of Jesus Christ been more organic, dynamic, life-filled, or powerful than in the first century. Oh yes, there have been revivals and movements of the Holy Spirit down through the centuries. But nothing as pure and Christ-filled as century one. So, this begs the question: Why is that? What was it that those believers had that we don't have? I have lived through several movements or revivals that I believe were from the Lord. I have also studied church his-tory quite extensively. But still, nothing emerges to be as Christ-filled and as Christ-centered as the story of the New Testament church in the first century. Oh, we have had many revivals and many movements. But I sincerely believe with all my heart that what is needed was nothing less than a revolu-tion! But the question that begs to be answered is: What did the first century Christian have that we are apparently missing today? To an-swer that question, we need to first take a quick look at what the first century believ-ers did not have.

They did *not* have technology.
Those believers couldn't just pull out their smart phones and call up any information or news in the world. They also could not look up

scripture, untold numbers of study helps, or Bible references on their laptops or cell phones. In fact, they had no phones at all.

They did *not* have transportation.
Those believers couldn't just hop on a plane and jet over to another country or another continent to share the gospel with others in a foreign land. They actually had to walk, which was a very perilous undertak-ing. There were murderous thieves along the roads. Of course, the Roman roads were good for that time and era—they went to all of the major cities.

They did *not* have adequate lodging.
There was some lodging in the form of inns, which in many cases were simply barns where cattle lived. There were also rooms for rent in various homes throughout the region. Probably most of the traveling workers (apostles) slept in bedrolls somewhere near the road yet concealed from robbers.

They did *not* have any media.
This may be difficult for us to understand, but the culture of the first century was not a culture of litera-ture. There were no books or printing of any kind! The printing press took fifteen more centuries to be invented by Guttenburg. Whatever was "printed" had to be handwritten. They had no books, no radios, no television, and definitely no internet. It was totally a verbal culture. They told stories. And this leads to one of my most important points.

They did *not* have any Bibles.
Now at this juncture I need to make a very important point. *I am not making a case against the written scriptures.* I believe strongly in

the veracity and importance of the scriptures (both Old and New Testa-ments), as you will see in this book. No, instead I am making another point which should become clear soon. So, please hang in there with me.

At this juncture in history, the scrolls of the Old Testament were only available to the religious hierarchy of the Jewish nation. If there were any scrolls available locally, they would be kept under lock and key in the local synagogue. This would usually just be a partial copy of one of the books, such as Isaiah that Je-sus read when He walked into the synagogue in Nazareth.

The first document written for the New Testament was the letter to the Galatians (written by Paul, of course) twenty-three years after Pentecost. So, there were no scriptures available to the general public for the first twenty-plus years of the life of the church.

How in the world did the Church of Jesus Christ survive (and even thrive) without any written scriptures?

Have you ever thought about this? For over twenty years of the church there were no Christian writings whatsoever. And yet, there can be no argument that she grew and prospered both physically and spiritual-ly over that period of time. And please remember, after twenty-three years there was now only one letter written. It would take years for the other letters to be written, mostly by Paul, as he traveled and plant-ed churches.

But that's not all...

Ninety-four percent of the population was illiterate.

Even if there had been books available, only six percent of the population would be able to read them. And those people would have been the rich, educated elite. And remember that only the elite leaders of the Jewish faith had access to any scrolls. And those scrolls were few and far between.

Since there was no Bible written yet, that means that there were absolutely no Bible colleges. No Bible dictionaries, different translations, or Bible helps of any kind. No one held degrees in theology. There were no Bible scholars or theologians. Simply stated, there just were very few writings of any kind and very few people were literate. Stories and the like were communicated by the spoken word, not the writ-ten word. It was a verbal culture, not a printed one.

The Secret

The secret of the early church did not lie in their biblical acuity. It did not rely on their great intelligence or ferocious emotionalism. No, not at all. Their secret was in a totally different place. But where was it? What was it that made these believers so alive? What was it that caused the incredible growth of the church throughout the world? What was it that caused these churches and believers to have so much strength and power and downright guts? What was it that caused these early believers (and churches) to have so much life, vitality, and strength?

The answer can only be found in one place.

> Now as they observed the confidence of Peter and John and understood that they were uneducated and untrained men, they were amazed, and began to recognize them as *having been with Jesus* (Acts 4:13).

There it is. There is the key, the secret to it all! *They had been with Jesus*. They were not very educated or trained but they had spent time with Jesus the Christ. That is the key and that is the secret. These men knew how to live by an indwelling Christ. They knew Him deeply and intimately. They knew how to abide and fellowship with a Christ who lived inside of them.

> I am the vine, you are the branches; he who abides in Me and I in him, he bears much fruit, for apart from Me you can do nothing (John 15:5).

Now you might be thinking, "These men actually physically walked and talked with Jesus. They had an advantage that we don't have." But there was one man who totally blew that theory out of the water. Saul of Tarsus! He never met Jesus in the flesh. Neither did any of the saints in the churches that Paul planted. Neither did Apollos, Barnabas, Timothy, Titus, or any of the other brothers who worked with Paul. No, the answer must lie in the fact that Christ lived in them and they knew how to abide in Him. This *indwelling* Christ is the secret!

Let me say that again: **This *indwelling* Christ is the secret!**

And that, dear reader, is the purpose of this book. My earnest desire in writing is to help you to know this indwelling Christ and then how to live by His life every day. May the Lord Jesus Christ reveal Himself to you as you read through and absorb the content of these pages. And may that Life be expressed and dis-played on this earth again as in the days of old.

PART ONE

Who is this Christ?

*"God...hath shined into our hearts to give the light of the knowl-
edge of the glory of God in the face of Jesus Christ"
(2 Cor. 4:6).*

the face of Jesus Christ
the glory of God in the face of Jesus Christ
the knowledge of the glory of God in the face of Jesus Christ
the light of the knowledge of the glory of God in the face of Jesus Christ
In our hearts the light of the knowledge of the glory of God in the face of
Jesus Christ

T. Austin-Sparks in "God Hath Spoken"

Chapter One

God's Eternal Purpose in Christ

I think chapter one would be a good place to start, don't you agree? However, when we are referring to God and His eternal purpose in Christ we actually have to begin somewhere other than the beginning. We must begin *before* the beginning. Now, this is a good place to ask for spiritual insight and understanding—the mind will be of no help here. The intellect is way too limited. We can only understand these things spiritually. Please do not even try to intellectually analyze these things. Just read them, then take them to the Lord and ask Him for the spiritual understanding. It will come, at the proper time, by the spirit of wisdom and revelation in the knowledge of Him.

> But a natural man does not accept the things of the Spirit of God, for they are foolishness to him; and he cannot understand them, because they are spiritually appraised (1 Corinthians 2:14).

Before we can look at this most sacred of places, that is, *before* the beginning, we need to understand why it is so difficult for us to see all of this.

The Typical Places Where We Begin

When we are endeavoring to understand God's eternal purpose in Christ we must absolutely be sure to begin at the correct place. The beginning is everything! Most Christians have never even heard of God's eternal purpose, yet it is all over the New Testament. Paul especially writes about this in his letters to the Colossians, Ephesians, Galatians, and various places throughout Corinthians and Romans. Peter and John also refer to this purpose throughout their writings. And, of course, Jesus speaks of His Father's purpose especially in the gospel of John.

Most Christians today are surprisingly ignorant of these things. And yet, the eternal purpose is the foundation for all of God's motivation for creation and all of His works.

So, let's first take a quick look at the usual ways that believers today look at God's purpose.

Through the Lens of Redemption

Starting with redemption as the beginning is what I call the "evangelical filter." This is the idea that the reason God created and sent His Son is to save (or redeem) mankind. This is probably by far the most popular "lens" for God's purpose and the place where many begin. So, we need to ask the most obvious question: Did God send His Son primarily to save humankind from our sins? It's clear that humankind did fall into sin in the garden in Genesis chapter three. But can we honestly say that God created humankind to save him from sin? Yes, humans sinned, but that didn't happen until chapter three. What happened in chapter one?

> Then God said, 'Let Us make mankind in Our image, according to Our likeness; and let them rule over the fish of the sea and over the birds of the sky and over the cattle and over all the earth, and over every creeping thing that creeps on the earth.' God created mankind in His own image, in the image of God He created him; male and female He created them (Genesis 1:26-27).

We can see from this passage in chapter one that God created mankind to be His image and likeness and to rule or have dominion on the earth. This is *before* the fall. Here we can clearly see God's original intention for mankind. But that's not all. The text reads, "Let Us make man in *Our* image." Here, God is speaking in plural pronouns. He is speaking here as a corporate (plural, yet one) God. And this is our key to the beginning of understanding His eternal purpose.

Through the Lens of Creation and Commission

The lens of creation and commission has Christians rallying around the fact that our God is a creator and commissioned mankind to be fruitful and multiply. Even though these things are true, God's original intention and motivation for creating and commissioning is something much deeper. The creation and the commission are not the primary things. Christians who focus on this lens are all into reclamation and restoration. Healing, miracles, faith, and prosperity are all part of the agenda for "ruling" on the earth.

However, God doesn't execute His purpose in this way. You see in Genesis chapter one verses 26-28, there is something that comes first, before the fruitfulness, multiplication, and finally the ruling or dominion.

The Proper Lens

So, what then is God's viewpoint and His purpose? What is the primary thing? The primary thing has everything to do with the *image*. Let's read the beginning of verse twenty-six again very carefully:

> God said, "Let Us [Father, Son, and Holy Spirit] make mankind in Our image, after Our likeness." (Genesis 1:26a).

The first thing He spoke of was His image, and everything that comes after that is secondary and as a result of the image. He only executes His purpose through an image. Now, we are getting to the heart of the matter. Now, we are going back to *before* the beginning. Before creation, before time and space, before the universe, before the spiritual realm, before eternity!

"God said, Let Us..."

Now, we need to understand when and where we are in the story. We are definitely *before*. That tells us *when*. But *where* are we? Remember, nothing has been created yet. In fact, nothingness has not even been created yet. I know this may blow your mind, but that is exactly what is needed.

If this *before* is a place and time before anything, then we can only arrive at one conclusion: *where* must be in God Himself. That's because before the beginning there is nothing else but God!

God is all.

Now, we need to ask the all-important question: What was going on inside the living God?

Some of you may be thinking: *Milt, what are you trying to do here? How can we know what God was doing before creation? Maybe it's none of our business! Maybe this is too holy and sacred of a thing for us mere mortals to know.*

Actually, the scripture is not silent about this. Jesus Himself spoke about His life with the Father before anything was created. Let's take a quick look at some of those references. (Please note that all of these passages of scripture have to do with the relationship, fellowship, and communion that was going on inside of the Godhead—Father, Son, Spirit—before creation.)

And now, Father, glorify Me along with Yourself and restore Me to such majesty and honor in Your presence as I had with You before the world existed (John 17:5).

I ask on their behalf; I do not ask on behalf of the world, but of those whom You have given Me; for they are Yours; and all things that are Mine are Yours, and Yours are Mine; and I have been glorified in them (John 17:9-10).

Father, I desire that they also, whom You have given Me, be with Me where I am, so that they may see My glory which You have given Me, for You loved Me before the foundation of the world (John 17:24).

All things have been handed over to Me by My Father; and no one knows the Son except the Father; nor does anyone know the Father except the Son, and anyone to whom the Son wills to reveal Him (Matthew 11:27).

Then a voice came out of the cloud, saying, "This is My Son, My Chosen One; listen to Him! (Luke 9:35).

For He was foreknown before the foundation of the world, but has appeared in these last times for the sake of you (1 Peter 1:20).

And all those dwelling in the earth will worship it, those of whom the names had not been written in the Book of Life of the Lamb having been slain from the foundation of the world (Revelation 13:8).

In the beginning was the Word, and the Word was with God, and the Word was God. He was in the beginning with God (John 1:1-2).

Blessed is the God and Father of our Lord Jesus Christ, who blessed us with every spiritual blessing in the heavenlies with Christ, even as He elected us in Him before the foundation of the world, for us to be holy and without blemish before Him in love, predestinating us to adoption through Jesus Christ to Himself, according to the good pleasure of His will (Ephesians 1:3-5).

But an hour is coming, and now is, when the true worshipers will worship the Father in spirit and in truth. For the Father also seeks such, the ones worshiping Him (John 4:23).

...but the Comforter, the Holy Spirit, whom the Father will send in My name, He shall teach you all things and shall remind you of all things that I said to you (John 14:26).

And when the Comforter comes, whom I will send to you from the Father, the Spirit of Truth who proceeds from the Father, that One will witness concerning Me (John 15:26).

Father, I desire that those whom You have given Me, that where I am, they may be with Me also, that they may behold My glory which You gave Me, because You loved Me before the foundation of the world (John 17:24).

I suggest you read the above scriptures several times. But I also recommend that you sit down one day and read the gospel of John chapters 14-17 without stopping (you may want to do this several times, as well). This is the last discourse that Jesus left his disciples before leaving the planet. You will begin to see the incredible and much-more-than-amazing fellowship that was (and is) happening between the Father, the Son, and the Spirit.

The grace of the Lord Jesus Christ and the love of God and the fellowship of the Holy Spirit be with you all. Amen (2 Corinthians 13:14).

...and to bring to light all, what is the fellowship of the mystery having been hidden from eternity in God, the One creating all things through Jesus Christ... (Ephesians 3:9).

My dear brothers and sisters, there was a holy and most sacred fellowship (communion) happening inside of your God way before there was anything created. That communion is the lifestyle of the Godhead. Now, drawing from the revelation we get from those who came before us, let's outline (very plainly) what God was "doing" before creation.

The Divine Activity of the Godhead

Before the beginning:

- The Father, Son, and Spirit were enjoying incredible fellowship.
- The Father was loving the Son—He was pouring out all of His life, love, and all to His Son.
- The Son was receiving all of this glorious love of the Father.
- This was all happening by and through the Holy Spirit (you could say He's the conduit).
- The Father gave His life (that is, His *all*) to the Son. He did not hold back any bit of His life for Himself, but rather, gave it all (without reservation or hesitation) to His Son. There was no fear of loss involved in this giving whatsoever. The Father did not hold back a "reserve" for Himself just in case. No! He gave it all, no holds barred, to the Son. You could say that the Father laid down all of His life for the Son.
- The Son then received this life very graciously and thankfully.

But that's not all:

- The Son then began to live by the life of His Father. Can you image? Choosing to life by the life of another even though you have your own life?

- Now both the Father and the Son are living by the same life (although "now" really doesn't exist in this instance because time itself is irrelevant). This exchange of divine life and love is all taking place through and in the Holy Spirit. And the joy. Oh, what a joy unspeakable and full of glory!

And now something even more incredible takes place:

- The Son takes this life that was given to Him so completely by the Father and He gives it back to the Father! In other words, the Son now lays down His life completely by giving it over to the Father.
- The Father now receives this life from the Son. But something has changed. Now the Father's life is flavored and blended with the life of the Son. And because the oneness is done through the agency of the Spirit, He is also combined within the mix.

Now, there are some things that we need to keep in mind here:

1. My description above is really lame! It's incredibly difficult to describe something which is absolutely indescribable.
2. While it sounds like this life within the Godhead happened either sequentially or as a one-time experience, neither of those things is true. It's like an eternal river flowing inside of God without end. The scriptures describe this as the *river of life*. This river has been flowing forever and will continue to flow forever.
3. The exchange of divine life and love is happening simultaneously. How can this be? I have no idea! But it's what is referred to in the scriptures as "eternal life."

4. Besides this exchange of divine life and love, there is another factor that can be overlooked and yet is incredibly important. The giving (or laying down) of the life of Father and the Son in the Spirit is something referred to in the scriptures as "the cross." Most believers see the cross as something wooden that Jesus hung upon when He was crucified. But spiritually it is so much more than that. This giving of life and love from one member of the Godhead to the other means a total giving of their lives for one another. Did you know that the Lamb of God was slain way before He died on the tree at Cavalry? "And all the inhabitants of the earth will be found to be worshiping him: every one whose name is not recorded in the Book of Life—the Book of the Lamb who has been offered in sacrifice ever since the creation of the world" (Revelation 13:8).

There it is! The Lamb was offered in sacrifice ever since the creation of the world. The cross is not just an event that happened two thousand years ago outside of Jerusalem, it is part of the very lifestyle of the living God. The Father, Son, and Holy Spirit have been completely laying down their lives for one another since before the eternals. Wow! What a life! What a community! What a fellowship!

Three persons who are so united in oneness that they can only be called **one** God! (There is much more than can be said about this community in God. You can read more about it in the authors' book *The Community Life of God*.)

A New Vision of the Image

Now, and only now, can we begin to understand what that one verse in Genesis 1:26 is really about.

> Then God said, "Let Us make man in Our image, according to Our likeness; and let them rule over the fish of the sea and over the birds of the sky and over the cattle and over all the earth, and over every creeping thing that creeps on the earth" (Genesis 1:26).

Can you now *begin* to understand? Can you now *begin* to see spiritually? This corporate (three-in-one) God said, "Let Us make man in Our image." This Triune God wanted a genuine representation and expression of His own community life. In fact, in this verse, the word *God* is the plural form of the Hebrew word *elohim*. It is a plural-in-one word! This God who is not an individualistic God but rather a community, wants a community among humans that shows who He is as a loving, sacrificing, giving, sharing, cross-bearing fellowship of many-who-are-*one*. They will be expressing His community, and not just because they do what He says, but because they live by His life!

Now many folks throughout the years have told me they want a model for the church. They claim that the model in the institutional church has been the wrong one. I definitely agree. However, they usually look for some other model. For example, they think the early church as portrayed in the scriptures should be our model. I disagree. Our model should be what *their* model was! And what was that model? It was nothing less than the community life of God Himself. You see, that is the true model. That is the *perfect* model. What we see happening in the book of Acts is not the model of the New Testament church—it is the very life of the triune God being lived out on the earth. It is eternal (divine) life being lived out by humans in Jerusalem, Samaria, Judea, Galatia, Asia, Greece, and so on. It is the life of Christ, the very same life that He is right now living inside the Godhead. It is the life of the head, Jesus Christ, being lived out by His body.

> Behold, how good and how pleasant it is for brethren to dwell together in unity! It is like the precious oil upon the head, coming down upon the beard, even Aaron's beard, coming down upon the edge of his robes. It is like the dew of Hermon coming down upon the mountains of Zion; For there the Lord commanded the blessing—life forever (Psalm 133:1-3).

The Eternal Purpose

Now we are getting down to what Paul called the *eternal purpose*.

> He made known to us the mystery of His will, according to His kind intention which He purposed in Him with a view to an administration suitable to the fullness of the times, that is, the summing up of all things in Christ, things in the heavens and things on the earth. In Him also we have obtained an inheritance, having been predestined according to His purpose who works all things after the counsel of His will, to the end that we who were the first to hope in Christ would be to the praise of His glory (Ephesians 1:9-12).

> I pray that the eyes of your heart may be enlightened, so that you will know what is the hope of His calling, what are the riches of the glory of His inheritance in the saints, and what is the

surpassing greatness of His power toward us who believe. These are in accordance with the working of the strength of His might which He brought about in Christ, when He raised Him from the dead and seated Him at His right hand in the heavenly places, far above all rule and authority and power and dominion, and every name that is named, not only in this age but also in the one to come. And He put all things in subjection under His feet, and gave Him as head over all things to the church, which is His body, the fullness of Him who fills all in all (Ephesians 1:18-23).

To me, the very least of all saints, this grace was given, to preach to the Gentiles the unfathomable riches of Christ, and to bring to light what is the administration of the mystery which for ages has been hidden in God who created all things; so that the manifold wisdom of God might now be made known through the church to the rulers and the authorities in the heavenly places. This was in accordance with the eternal purpose which He carried out in Christ Jesus our Lord... (Ephesians 3:8-11).

These verses from Paul have mystified Bible readers (and theologians!) for centuries. But when you read these passages (and many others) in light of God's motivation for creating the human race, it all begins to become clear. I have heard it said before that to understand the Bible you need to read the first two chapters (Genesis 1 & 2) and the last two chapters (Revelation 21 & 22) to see what God wanted (His purpose for man). That's because the first two chapters are *before* the fall of man and the last two chapters are *after* the fall of man. Everything in between these four chapters is about bringing humankind back to their original condition—and even beyond that. What if Adam and Eve would have partaken of the Tree of Life? Then they would have lived by God's own divine life (His community) and they would have fulfilled His purpose of having an image on the earth to express His life and rule over all things. It's interesting because if you read those four chapters in the very beginning and in the very ending of the Bible, you will see that they are remarkably similar. What God wanted in the very beginning He gets at the end! The New Jerusalem is the fulfillment of God's dream for His people. That is, a nation, a city, a civilization, a kingdom, a culture, and a society, that is being lived out by humans but by God's life in Christ. God used this people to conquer His enemies and bring His kingdom to the earth.

This, in a very small nutshell, is the Lord's eternal purpose. So, let me once again summarize all of this:

- God had an ultimate intention or purpose before He created anything. This eternal purpose is also referred to in the New Testament as the *mystery hidden before the ages* (Eph. 3:8-11; Col. 1:25-27).
- We see this mystery or purpose revealed when God first created mankind. God, speaking in the plural, creates mankind in His image to be fruitful and rule the earth (Gen. 1:26-28).
- While this has nothing to do with redemption, healing, miracles, ministry, or any of the other things Christians are always running after, mankind did fall and then needed redemption and restoration. Throughout history God is promising to send His Redeemer who would rescue mankind from his sins and himself. Then, Christ comes and accomplishes His awesome work.

- Christ is called the image of God (Col. 1:15) and therefore is the fulfillment of God's original intention and purpose.
- This Christ (when He is resurrected) is no longer a single seed/image but now becomes a whole harvest of grain! The one becomes many new grains (the church). He is now a corporate Christ who has many body parts (members). He is now a new nation, city, body, bride, family, house, warrior, and the new humanity.
- It is *this* Christ, and *only this* Christ who fulfills God's eternal purpose. It's *this Christ* in you and *this* Christ in me that fulfills the heart of the Father to have an image that truly reflects His nature, character, and authority.
- This is the reason why you were born. This is the reason why you were saved. This is the reason why you wake up every morning. This is the reason why you are breathing air. And this is the reason why you are reading this book right now!

There is so much more that can be shared about this glorious eternal purpose. It, quite literally, could fill the whole world with books. So, I recommend that when you finish with this book that you also read some of the books I list in the appendix.

Now that we have a basic knowledge of the eternal purpose of God, let's move on to a greater understanding and revelation of Jesus Christ.

Chapter Two

For I would have you know, brethren, that the gospel which was preached by me is not according to man. For I neither received it from man, nor was I taught it, but I received it through a revelation of Jesus Christ (Gal. 1:11-12).

...that the God of our Lord Jesus Christ, the Father of glory, may give to you a spirit of wisdom and of revelation in the [experiential] knowledge of Him (Eph. 1:17).

If there is one thing in scarcity among Christians today it is a deep *revelation* of the person of Jesus Christ. Most believers today know Him only as the savior, the redeemer, the healer, the miracle worker, the preacher, the deliverer, and the only begotten Son of God. While these titles and aspects of Him are all very fitting, He is so much more! We have hardly even begun to know our Lord. We haven't even begun to touch the surface of Him, let alone scratch it. He is *that* deep, and *that* wide, and *that* high, and *that* long.

> ...so that Christ may dwell in your hearts through faith; and that you, being rooted and grounded in love, may be able to comprehend with all the saints what is the breadth and length and height and depth...(Eph. 3:17-18).

We only know Him in relationship to *what He can do for us*. But does it always have to be about us?

I want to know Him according to who and what He really is, not according to my limited thoughts about Him. I want an unveiling of Him. I want the curtains of my own understanding, flesh, and religious mindset to be rolled back so that I can see Him as He truly is. Are you with me, dear reader?

> ...that I may know Him and the power of His resurrection and the fellowship of His sufferings, being conformed to His death; in order that I may attain to the resurrection from the dead (Phil. 3:10-11).

The Unlimited One

If I understand the New Testament writings correctly (especially those of Paul), then this Christ of ours is without limits and without borders. He is so vast, Paul tells us that His riches are unfathomable (without end).

To me, though I am the very least of all the saints [God's consecrated people], this grace [favor, privilege] was granted and graciously entrusted: to proclaim to the Gentiles the unending [boundless, fathomless, incalculable, and exhaustless] riches of Christ [wealth which no human being could have searched out] (Eph. 3:8).

Did you get that? The riches of our Christ are unending, boundless, fathomless, incalculable, and exhaustless (new word!). Wow! And those are just His riches. What else is located inside of this Christ? That would take a whole other book (or many books) to even begin to describe. But let's take a quick look at His riches.

Paul tells us that the riches of our Christ are unending. This means that they are, first of all, without measure. For example, the grace of God is unlimited. There is no end to how big this grace is and how long it will last. This grace is eternal. It's a huge grace! If you traveled inside of God's grace at the speed of light (186,000 miles per second), it would take you the rest of eternity to reach the end. And, of course, eternity itself is without end. So, we could also say that eternity is one of His riches.

What about His love?

Who shall ever separate us from Christ's love? Shall suffering and affliction and tribulation? Or calamity and distress? Or persecution or hunger or destitution or peril or sword? (Rom. 8:35).

God's boundless love in Christ has no borders and no boundaries. It is unlimited in all ways. God never runs out. And the quality of this love...oh! The quality is of the highest order. "Greater love has no one than this, that one lay down his life for his friends" (John 15:13). Did our Lord Jesus lay His life down for you and me? Yes, indeed! That is the exact same love that lives inside of you and me—the greatest, most perfect, eternal love of God that loves the whole world so much so that God Himself (in the flesh) laid down His life for all of us. You see, love is intrinsically tied to the cross of Christ. True divine love will never be expressed unless a life is laid down. This is a spiritual principle interwoven into the universe.

But what about hope?

Now may the God of hope fill you with all joy and peace in believing, so that you will abound in hope by the power of the Holy Spirit (Rom. 15:13).

And what about joy?

...for the kingdom of God is not eating and drinking, but righteousness and peace and joy in the Holy Spirit (Rom. 14:17).

And what about righteousness? Peace? Faith? Holiness? Truth? And freedom? Patience? Humility? Kindness? Wisdom? (Just to name a few.) These are all riches of our glorious Christ.

But wait...

There is much more depth to all of this than we can ever imagine. There are actually riches *within* riches. How can this be? Paul tells us this:

> In Him we have redemption through His blood, the forgiveness of our trespasses, according to the *riches of His grace* (Eph. 1:7).

> ...so that in the ages to come He might show the surpassing *riches of His grace* in kindness toward us in Christ Jesus (Eph. 2:7).

Grace is one of God's riches in Christ, and yet Paul tells us that there are more riches inside of grace. So here we have riches *within* riches! How many riches are inside of His unending grace? I have no idea, but I have a feeling that those riches within riches are also without limits and without boundaries.

When we are referring to God's fullness inside of the Unlimited One (who is Christ), we have to realize that there is much more to Him than just riches.

The Image of God

> He is the image of the invisible God, the firstborn of all creation. For by Him all things were created, both in the heavens and on earth, visible and invisible, whether thrones or dominions or rulers or authorities—all things have been created through Him and for Him. He is before all things, and in Him all things hold together (Col. 1:15-17).

God wanted to have an image. This means that He wanted to have a physical expression of Himself. God Himself is spirit (John 4:24) but He created a physical universe and wanted to have a physical expression or image of Himself. This image is Jesus Christ. When the triune God created mankind, He did so with Christ in mind. God (Father, Son, Spirit) wanted to create an expression of who He is and how He lives. This God of ours is three Persons who are one, the very definition of community. Each person totally lives for the others and not for Himself. There is a total laying down of their own lives for the others. There is a total giving. There is a total consideration for the others first. This is the love of God!

When God became a man in Jesus Christ, He showed us this love as the true image of God. The Son continued to do what He had always done in the community of the Godhead: He laid down His life! Not only that, but all of the character, power, and wisdom of God was (and still is) expressed in and through Jesus.

> For indeed Jews ask for signs and Greeks search for wisdom; but we preach Christ crucified, to Jews a stumbling block and to Gentiles foolishness, but to those who are the called, both Jews and Greeks, Christ the power of God and the wisdom of God (1 Cor. 1:22-24).

The Center of Creation

Colossians also tells us that Christ is the *firstborn* of all creation. And that by Him, *through* Him, and *for* Him all things were created. That He is before all things and in Him all things hold together. Do you see it, dear saint? All things. All things. *All things*! What a glorious Lord. What an incredibly full Christ.

The Firstborn

> We look at this Son and see the God who cannot be seen. We look at this Son and see God's original purpose in everything created. For everything, absolutely everything, above and below, visible and invisible, rank after rank after rank of angels—everything got started in Him and finds its purpose in Him (Col. 1:15-16).

Here again, we see the idea of Christ being the image of God. The Son expresses the invisible God. He makes God visible so that we humans can understand Him. But also, we can see God's original purpose in Christ. Why did God create all that you see?

Simply put, it is for this reason: that there would be a visible expression of His Son in this physical and spiritual universe. Jesus Christ is the image of God. But let us know and remember that Jesus of Nazareth went through some changes. First of all, the eternal Son became a human being. This is referred to theologically as the incarnation. As John tells us in his gospel, the Word became flesh and dwelt among us (John 1:14). (This whole section in John from 1:1-18 is a great companion passage to Colossians 1:15-16.)

But that's not all!

This Christ was also crucified. He went through rejection, ridicule, persecution, slander, and ultimately abuse, both physical and emotional. His cross was the great eliminator. This one act of surrender to the Father's will accomplished so much. Sin was crucified on this cross. The old man was crucified on this cross. The devil and all his angels were defeated on this cross. The whole old creation was crucified on this cross. The law was crucified on this cross. Death itself was also crucified on this cross (which itself was an instrument of death). Oh yes, and don't let me forget one more—you were also crucified on this cross!

The seed fell into the ground (of His own accord) and died.

But that's not all!

This Christ was also resurrected on the third day. Yes! And when the seed came up out of death He did not rise alone. Please read that line again very carefully: When the seed came up out of death He did not rise alone.

> I assure you, most solemnly I tell you, Unless a grain of wheat falls into the earth and dies, it remains [just one grain; it never becomes more but lives] by itself alone. But if it dies, it produces many others and yields a rich harvest (John 12:24).

Brothers and sisters, let me ask you who are the "many others" and the "rich harvest" that our Lord is referring to here? It's you! It's me! It's all the saints! Jesus went into the grave alone, but He rose up with all of the members of His body inside of Him! He is now a corporate Christ, as Paul so beautifully portrays for us in his writings.

> For those whom He foreknew, He also predestined to become conformed to the image of His Son, so that He would be the firstborn among many brethren (Rom. 8:29).

The firstborn among *many* brethren. Our Christ is now a many-membered Christ. That's because He has a many-membered body

(1 Cor. 12:12). The head *and* the body make up one person. That is the person that Paul is referring to when he uses the word *Christ*.

But that's not all!

Since all things were created in Him, by Him, and through Him, this precludes that He is the forerunner or the "model" of creation. If the Father was compared to the master painter, and creation as the canvas, then the model for the artwork would be His Son! That means that everything He created reveals something about His Son.

All Things Were Created by Him

God created all things *by* Christ. Here we see that all of creation, visible and invisible, was brought into being by the direct intervention of the Son of God. Please realize that this verse is not just speaking of the visible creation. But let's take that aspect for the moment. Just think about the physical universe. Do we even know how big this universe is? Well, no one seems to know for sure, but some scientists say that the radius is about 46 billion light years. Since light travels at the speed of 186,000 miles per second, it would take 46 billion of those years to travel across it! But that's not all. That is just the size of the observable universe. This means that we can only see this part with of it with the Hubble telescope. It is actually much larger than this, and some believe it is infinite.

Now get this: Paul tells us that this visible creation was created inside of Jesus Christ!

And not only that, but this creation was created *through* Him, that is, executed by the agency of this person. Also, in Him all things hold together. You could say that this Christ is the "glue" that holds the physical universe together. Wow! But we are not done yet. There is another part of the creation.

The Invisible Creation

The invisible creation refers to the spiritual or heavenly realms. They did not always exist; they were created at some point. We don't know a lot about these realms, but we do know that there are beings that inhabit these realms. They are referred to in scripture as angels, cheribim, seriphim, sons of God, principalities, powers, etc. We know that they have different tasks depending upon the type of angelic being. Archangels are the highest and most powerful. They are used by God to protect His people on earth, send messages, and proclaim His glory in heaven.

What else is in this realm besides the inhabitants? We really don't know. How big are these realms? We really don't know. However, I have a feeling that these realms are even larger than the visible universe. But here is my point: Both the *visible* and the *invisible* realms are inside of your glorious Lord! (You may have to read that last sentence again.)

Again, the purpose for all of this is not that God was bored and decided to one day create so that He would have something to do. It's so that everything would find its purpose in Christ.

But wait, there is more...

The Church

> He is also head of the body, the church; and He is the beginning, the firstborn from the dead, so that He Himself will come to have first place in everything. For it was the Father's good pleasure for all the fullness to dwell in Him, and through Him to reconcile all things to Himself, having made peace through the blood of His cross; through Him, I say, whether things on earth or things in heaven (Colossians 1:18-20).

Christ is the head of the body, the church. The word "head" here is *kephale* in the Greek language and literally means *life source*. It also implies authority. So, we have a head that is the life-source and authority of the body. He is the authority because He is also the life-source. The body functions and expresses the Head because it is the very life of the Head whereby the body lives.

This totally redefines our definition of *church*. The church is Christ personified. She is the expression of the head. If there is a disconnection from the head, then the body is not really being the body. The body cannot be who she is without the life source and life flow of the head.

This is also true within the human body from which model Paul is drawing his correlation. Of course, the body must be in harmony with the head. But the body must also be in harmony with the rest of the body! The whole person must function by the same life and the same oneness. Did you know that when the human brain makes a decision it sends a signal to every part of the body before execution? It uses the nervous system to convey this signal, and it goes to every part, even to every single cell. That's because the life of the head must flow into all of the body. When this doesn't happen then you have something which is referred to as disease or dis-ease.

Firstborn from the Dead

In Colossians 1:15, Christ is referred to as the *firstborn of creation*. Then, in verse 18 He is referred to as the *firstborn from the dead*. This is in reference to His resurrection. In correlation to this, Romans 8:29 says He is firstborn among many brethren. Because of His victory in resurrection, He was made the firstborn among many brethren (the church). Christ, in overcoming sin, the devil, the world system, the religious system, the flesh, and death itself, qualified Himself to become the head of a whole new creation and humanity called the *ekklesia*.

Then, Paul tells us the goal and purpose for all of this: "...so that He alone in everything and in every respect might occupy the chief place [stand first and be preeminent]" (Col. 1:18).

God's goal is always to make His Son preeminent in all things and in all ways. That is the *purpose*, but the *method* is the church!

Fullness

It was the Father's good pleasure for all the fullness to dwell in Christ. But what fullness? All of the fullness of everything that Paul describes in verses 15-17 of Colossians. *All* of the visible creation. *All* of the invisible creation. *All* of the fullness of the Godhead. One translation puts it this way: "For it has pleased [the Father] that all the divine fullness (the sum total of the divine perfection, powers, and attributes) should dwell in Him permanently" (Col. 1:19).

But that's not all!

Here there is not Greek and Jew, circumcised and uncircumcised, barbarian, Scythian, slave, free; but Christ is all, and in all (Colossians 3:11).

In reference to the church, the *ekklesia*, Paul tells us that Christ *is all* and *in all*. He not only has the fullness inside of Him, but that same Christ (who has the fullness) lives inside of every true believer in His *ekklesia*. That makes Him the all in all! Dear reader, if you have been born from above by the Spirit of God then you are part of that "all!" And you have Christ (and His fullness) living inside of you!

Reconciliation

> ...and through Him to reconcile all things to Himself, having made peace through the blood of His cross; through Him, I say, whether things on earth or things in heaven... (Col. 1:20).

> For I calculate that the sufferings of the present time are not worthy to compare to the coming glory to be revealed in us. For the earnest expectation of the creation eagerly awaits the revelation of the sons of God. For the creation was not willingly subjected to vanity, but through Him subjecting it, on hope; that also the creation will be freed from the slavery of corruption to the freedom of the glory of the children of God (Rom. 8:18-21).

The whole creation fell into corruption when mankind fell. Yet all of creation (visible and invisible) will be reconciled to God through His beloved Son. And isn't it wonderful that because the corruption came in through mankind that it is through a Christ-centered, Christ-redeemed humanity that creation will be redeemed! This all takes place *in Christ.*

Chapter Three

The Misunderstanding of Metaphors

I am the Vine—the True Vine, and my Father is the vine-dress-
er (John 15:1).

The word *true* in this verse literally means "the real" or "genuine." Do you see what your Lord is saying here? He is telling us that He is the *real vine.* He is the *original* vine. He is the *genuine article,* as we say. All concepts of a vine come from Him: the first, the genuine, and the only *real* vine!

Now, please pay attention to this: the physical grapevine that you can see with your physical eyes in a physical vineyard is *not* the real vine. The real vine is Christ! He existed as a vine before creation. He was a vine to His Father in the Spirit. He provided the true food and true drink to the Father through the Spirit. And the Father was a vine to Him, as well.

When Jesus was walking around the shores of the sea of Galilee and speaking, He was not just coming up with cute metaphors to illustrate His messages. He was speaking the reality of who He is inside of God. He was saying: I am, *I am,* **I am!** He was speaking from His own experiences in eternity with the living God. As I shared in chapter two, the physical creation came out of a vision God had within the invisible realm. The Father used His Son as a model for the physical creation. That was part of the Son's role as the *firstborn* of creation.

> Therefore let no one sit in judgment on you in matters of food and drink, or with regard to a feast day or a New Moon or a Sabbath. Such [things] are only the shadow of things that are to come, and they have only a symbolic value. But the reality (the substance, the solid fact of what is foreshadowed, the body of it) belongs to Christ (Col. 2:16-17).

One of the many aspects of His Son is that He is a vine. This is not metaphoric language here—He *is* the vine. The physical vine is a "picture" or "shadow" of the substance, who is Christ.

In the paragraphs to come we will be using such shadows to help us understand more of the fullness of who this Christ actually is. In this area we are standing on the ground of eternity—there is no way that any book could contain all of the descriptions, shadows, and pictures of an unlimited Christ. Here we will simply take a look at those descriptions He used to describe Himself while on the earth.

How can we describe this Christ? Let us count the ways...

The Word of God

> In the beginning [before all time] was the Word (Christ), and the
> Word was with God, and the Word was God Himself (John 1:1).

We know that this *Word* is Jesus Christ, not only because of this
one verse, but also because of the proceeding verses.

> He was present originally with God. All things were made and
> came into existence through Him; and without Him was not
> even one thing made that has come into being. In Him was life,
> and the life was the light of men (John 1:2-4).

This *Word* that John is describing is a *He* and a *Him*, making it
clear that the Word is a person. We also can see that this person must
be divine because all things were made in Him. Sound familiar? Kind
of like Colossians chapter one? Apparently, John and Paul were on the
same page here. But of course, that's not all.

In verse fourteen of chapter one we see much more:

> And the Word (Christ) became flesh (human, incarnate) and
> tabernacled (fixed His tent of flesh, lived awhile) among us; and
> we [actually] saw His glory (His honor, His majesty), such glory
> as an only begotten son receives from His Father, full of grace
> (favor, loving-kindness) and truth (John 1:14).

And in Revelation:

> His eyes are a flame of fire, and on His head are many dia-
> dems; and He has a name written on Him which no one knows
> except Himself. He is clothed with a robe dipped in blood, and
> His name is called The Word of God (Rev. 19:12-13).

Also, in Revelation 1:8 He is called the Alpha and Omega. As you may know, Alpha is the first letter of the Greek alphabet and Omega is the last letter of the Greek alphabet. This is another example of Him being the Word—He is the first letter and the last letter. For the English-speaking world this would translate into the fact that He is the A and the Z. And every letter in between as well. He is the alphabet. He is all of the tools and building blocks of language. And if He is the Word of God, then that means that He is the only tool of communication (language) that God the Father (through the Holy Spirit) uses.

A word is the smallest part of any language. But He is not just a word, He is all of the words. But of which language? God's language!

Hence, the title *Word of God*. This Christ is the very language or communication tool of the living God. In other words, when God speaks, it's Christ! God only speaks one language: His beloved Son. If you want to know God, the only way to do that is in and through Christ. There is no other way to communicate to the Father except through the Son. If you are speaking any other language but Christ, God simply cannot (and will not) hear you. And God will only speak to you by and through His Son. This why He told us: "This is My beloved Son, with whom I am well-pleased; listen to Him!" (Matthew 17:5).

The Genuine Tabernacle

In John chapter one verse fourteen we are told that the Word became flesh and *dwelt* among us. The literal translation of the word dwelt is "tabernacled." Of course, that is not an ordinary English word but that's the actual translation. The Word tabernacled among us. This gives us a clue to something. Our Christ is the genuine tabernacle! The tent that was carted around and set-up by the Hebrew nation traveling through the wilderness was a picture or shadow of Christ. We don't have the space or time to get into the intricacies of this particular shadow, but let's take a quick look at some of the main features.

- The tabernacle was set-up at the center of the encampment of the nation of Israel representing that this Christ is to be the very center and heart of God's people.
- The tabernacle was comprised of three sections: the outer court, the holy place, and the holy of holies. This points to the fact that Christ is the fullness of the Godhead; Father, Son, and Holy Spirit.
- The ark of the covenant (in the center of the tabernacle in the holy of holies) contains three items: the manna (Christ), the stone tablet of the law (Father), and the rod that budded (Holy Spirit). The ark itself is also Christ who contains the fullness of the Godhead.
- All of the materials used to create the tabernacle also represent Christ in His nature and work.
- The priesthood is a shadow of our great High Priest, Jesus Christ, and His church who are a kingdom of priests unto God.

- All of the offerings administered by the priests represent the cross of Christ, His nature, and His work of redemption and reconciliation.
- The tribes of Israel encamped around the tabernacle in the shape of a cross.

And this glorious tabernacle lived and moved among us. And guess what? He still does—in and through His church.

The Lamb of God

The next day he saw Jesus coming to him and said, "Behold, the Lamb of God who takes away the sins of the world!" (John 1:29).

It's very interesting to me that John the Baptist said this introductory remark about our Lord. The way that it is presented is almost like he was announcing, "Here He is, folks!" But notice that he calls Him the *Lamb of God*. Why not the Redeemer? Why not the Savior? Why not Prophet, Holy One of Israel, Son of the living God? The title *Lamb of God* is extremely pregnant with meaning. It is the title used extensively (32 times) throughout the book of the Revelation of Jesus Christ. Let's take a look at just a few of those references.

When He had taken the book, the four living creatures and the twenty-four elders fell down before the Lamb, each one holding a harp and golden bowls full of incense, which are the prayers of the saints (Rev. 5:8).

...saying with a loud voice, "Worthy is the Lamb that was slain to receive power and riches and wisdom and might and honor and glory and blessing" (Rev. 5:12).

After these things I looked, and behold, a great multitude which no one could count, from every nation and all tribes and peoples and tongues, standing before the throne and before the Lamb, clothed in white robes, and palm branches were in their hands; and they cry out with a loud voice, saying, "Salvation to our God who sits on the throne, and to the Lamb" (Rev. 7:9-10).

I said to him, "My lord, you know." And he said to me, "These are the ones who come out of the great tribulation, and they have washed their robes and made them white in the blood of the Lamb. For this reason, they are before the throne of God; and they serve Him day and night in His temple; and He who sits on the throne will spread His tabernacle over them" (Rev. 7:14-15).

So, brothers and sisters, there we have it. At the end, at the consummation of all things, when the kingdom of this world becomes the kingdom of our Lord and of His Christ (Rev. 11:15), we see that the most common name this Christ has is a *Lamb*! But not just any lamb, but the Lamb of the living God. He is called by many other titles in this final letter, but the Lamb is the most common. Can you imagine why? Why aren't the titles used most in this letter those of total dominion and sovereignty, such as *King of kings* and *Lord of lords*? I mean, this letter is all about the end and how the Lord Jesus will be victor over all.

And yet, at the center (in the midst) of the throne of God there is a Lamb! "...for the Lamb in the center of the throne will be their shepherd, and will guide them to springs of the water of life; and God will wipe every tear from their eyes" (Rev. 7:17).

This speaks incredible volumes as to who our Lord is and how He overcame. He overcame and now rules all things because of His nature as a little lamb. Think about the life and nature of a physical little lamb. Can you think of a more innocent creature? Can you think of a weaker and more defenseless creature? Sheep have absolutely no defenses against predators. They are also easily led by the Shepherd. They know how to follow. They know how to submit. They know the shepherd's voice and only follow that voice. Wow! The nature of our Lord is beautifully portrayed by a sweet, defenseless, and innocent lamb. He was willing to become the least, the last, and the lowest. He was willing to be shamed and rejected by men, yet actually being the Lord of all glory. And there, yes there, is the victory, my friends. There, yes there, is the power of it all. The power of the cross.

> For the word of the cross is foolishness to those who are perishing, but to us who are being saved it is the power of God (1 Cor. 1:18).

> ...few will be the lovers...within this painting...few will be the lovers of his cross.
> ("Few Be the Lovers" by John Michael Talbot)

The Heavenly Ladder

> Then Jacob departed from Beersheba and went toward Haran. He came to a certain place and spent the night there, because the sun had set; and he took one of the stones of the place and put it under his head, and lay down in that place. He had a dream, and behold, a ladder was set on the earth with its top reaching to heaven; and behold, the angels of God were ascending and descending on it. And behold, the LORD stood above it and said, "I am the LORD, the God of your father Abraham and the God of Isaac; the land on which you lie, I will give it to you and to your descendants" (Gen. 28:10-13).

> Nathanael answered Him, "Rabbi, You are the Son of God; You are the King of Israel." Jesus answered and said to him, "Because I said to you that I saw you under the fig tree, do you believe? You will see greater things than these." And He said to him, "Truly, truly, I say to you, you will see the heavens opened and the angels of God ascending and descending on the Son of Man" (John 1:49-51).

You may have never heard this before, but our Lord Jesus is the ladder, the stairway, the doorway between heaven and earth. There are many aspects to this description of our Lord. He is the way to the Father: "Jesus said to him, 'I am the way, and the truth, and the life; no one comes to the Father but through Me'" (John 14:6). He is the great Connector between heaven and earth. He is the conduit between the physical realm and the spiritual one. He is the only pathway from heaven to earth and from earth to heaven.

Now this may sound strange to you at first but think about it. Remember that we saw in Colossians chapter one that the whole creation (visible and invisible) exists inside of Him? Friends, I have no idea how that works, but I do know that it is absolutely true. If you can see (by revelation) that Christ encompasses all of creation, then why would it be a huge stretch to see Him also as the ladder from one realm to the other? Both realms are already inside of Him. What a huge Christ!

Now, let me pose an even crazier question to you: How do you enter the heavenly realms? Most evangelical Christians would say, "you have to physically die." But is "heaven" the same thing as the "heavenly places" that Paul talks about?

There are five references in the New Testament for the exact phrase of "heavenly places," and they are all found in Paul's letter to the Ephesians.

> Blessed be the God and Father of our Lord Jesus Christ, who has blessed us with every spiritual blessing in the heavenly places in Christ (Eph. 1:3).

> ...which He brought about in Christ, when He raised Him from the dead and seated Him at His right hand in the heavenly places (Eph. 1:20).

> ...and raised us up with Him, and seated us with Him in the heavenly places in Christ Jesus (Eph. 2:6).

> ...so that the manifold wisdom of God might now be made known through the church to the rulers and the authorities in the heavenly places (Eph. 3:10).

> For our struggle is not against flesh and blood, but against the rulers, against the powers, against the world forces of this darkness, against the spiritual forces of wickedness in the heavenly places (Eph. 6:12).

My purpose here is not to give you a complete study or even revelation on the heavenlies, but just to whet your appetites for what is to come later on in this book. For now, let's just say the following from the scriptures we have perused.

- Jesus Christ (the Word of God) is the only doorway between heaven and earth (Gen. 28:10-13 and John 1:49-51).
- The heavenly places and the physical creations are inside of Christ (Col. 1:16,17).
- This extremely full Christ lives inside of all believers (Col. 1:26, 27).
- Every true Christian has (past tense) received the spiritual blessings which are in Christ (Eph. 1:3).
- We are (right now) seated with Him in the heavenly places (Eph. 2:6).

Suffice it to say that every one of these truths have tremendous implications. You may be thinking, "Oh Milt, please, you have gone too far this time!" But is it possible to go too far when we are speaking of this gloriously endless and unlimited Christ? I say, "No! A thousand times no!"

The New Wine

> When the wine ran out, the mother of Jesus said to Him, "They
> have no wine" (John 2:3).

Doesn't it make sense that if Jesus is the true vine then He is also the true *wine*? He is not only the instrument (vine) but He is also the product or result (wine). He is the source, but He is also the fruit thereof. He is all! The vine, the branches, the root, the leaves, the fruit, the soil, the rain, etc.

At the wedding of Cana, the cheap wine ran out. This is man's best attempts at being holy, good, and religious—it runs out quickly. The best that man can do is like water. This is like the human spirit. The spirit of man cannot produce anything of value because the whole being (spirit, soul, and body) is fallen. But what if a new element could be added to the human spirit to give him new life?

> Jesus answered, "Truly, truly, I say to you, unless one is born
> of water and the Spirit he cannot enter into the kingdom of
> God. That which is born of the flesh is flesh, and that which is
> born of the Spirit is spirit" (John 3:5-6).

This is the new wine! The Spirit of God coming to dwell within a dead pot of clay. Now, His Spirit is living within your spirit and the two have become one. "But the one who joins himself to the Lord is one spirit with Him" (1 Cor. 6:17). Jesus Christ is the new wine that is poured out into our spirits so that we can know Him and He can live His life in and through us.

The Bridegroom

It is so fitting that your Lord performs His first miracle at a wedding. Think about it. A wedding! There is a bridegroom and a bride. The wine is there to provide drink for this new couple, in celebration of their love for one another.

The Temple of God

> Jesus answered them, "Destroy this temple, and in three days I will raise it up" (John 2:19).

> In My Father's house are many dwelling places; if it were not so, I would have told you; for I go to prepare a place for you. If I go and prepare a place for you, I will come again and receive you to Myself, that where I am, there you may be also (John 14:2-3).

> However, the Most High does not dwell in houses made by human hands; as the prophet says: "Heaven is my throne, and earth is the footstool of my feet; what kind of house will you build for me?" says the Lord, "Or what place is there for my repose? Was it not my hand which made all these things?" (Acts 7:48-50).

> If any man destroys the temple of God, God will destroy him, for the temple of God is holy, and that is what you are (1 Cor. 3:17).

> ...having been built on the foundation of the apostles and proph-
> ets, Christ Jesus Himself being the corner stone, in whom the
> whole building, being fitted together, is growing into a holy tem-
> ple in the Lord, in whom you also are being built together into a
> dwelling of God in the Spirit (Eph. 2:20-22).

Jesus Christ is the dwelling place of God. The Father, Son, and Spirit all dwell in that place. He is the Father's house. The Father loves to live in this person (who is Christ). He loves to share all of His love and life with this Person. The Son is the environment of the Father. The Father lives and moves and breathes *in* the Son and *by* the Spirit. You might say that the Father lives in the house of His Son and the Spirit is the energy (electricity and water) or the utilities inside of that house. But remember, the Son and the Spirit are not inanimate things such as wood, nails, water, and electricity. They are living breathing persons. These things (such as the temple) are only shadows or pictures of spiritual realities. The persons are the substance. The community life of these three persons is the expression of the reality.

God lives as a family inside of this house.

You and I can experience these things on a human level. For example, you were probably born and raised in a house with your family. So, you can understand it (a little) when the Lord says that He is the Father's house. But...you have only experienced the shadow. You have not yet truly experienced the reality until you come to know the Lord as your dwelling place. And even then, your experience is still only one-dimensional. It's a wonderful thing to know (by spiritual experience) the Lord Jesus as your dwelling place.

But that's not all!

The fulfillment of the expression of God's dwelling place only comes as you experience Him as your dwelling *with other saints*. God's eternal purpose is not fulfilled by you having a personal relationship with your personal Lord. It is only fulfilled by the head and the body, the house, the family, the vine and the branches, the shepherd and the sheep, the bridegroom and the bride. Don't forget that God earnestly desires to have an image of the community life within the Godhead. This is a corporate life. This is a *life together*. Dear believers, this includes you and me.

Most Christians never even scratch the surface of the depths of this wondrous Christ. This has been written in an attempt to help remedy that situation. The goal of this book is not only to help you to know your Lord in greater depth, but also to help you understand and know (by experience) your Lord *in His body!*

Chapter Four

The Christ Who is More

In many separate revelations [each of which set forth a portion of the Truth] and in different ways God spoke of old to [our] forefathers in and by the prophets, [But] in the last of these days He has spoken to us in [the person of a] Son, Whom He appointed Heir and lawful Owner of all things, also by and through Whom He created the worlds and the reaches of space and the ages of time [He made, produced, built, operated, and arranged them in order]. He is the sole expression of the glory of God [the Light-being, the out-raying or radiance of the divine], and He is the perfect imprint and very image of [God's] nature, upholding and maintaining and guiding and propelling the universe by His mighty word of power. When He had by offering Himself accomplished our cleansing of sins and riddance of guilt, He sat down at the right hand of the divine Majesty on

high, [Taking a place and rank by which] He Himself became as
much superior to angels as the glorious Name (title) which He
has inherited is different from and more excellent than theirs.
(Hebrews 1:1-4)

The Center of Revelation

In this passage we can see that the Son of God is the center of the
thought and revelation of God in both Old and New Testaments.
God definitely has something on His mind and the scriptures reveal
this *thought of God*. That is why He spoke through the prophets in
the Old Testament. That is why He spoke through the apostles in the
New Testament. He has only one purpose and one thought: His Son
and the expression of His Son. In God's mind it is all about this person and the eventual full expression of this person. "You search the
scriptures because you think that in them you have eternal life; it is
these that testify about Me" (John 5:39).

The Heir of All Things

In these last days (the days of the New Covenant), God has appointed
this Son as the heir and lawful owner of all things. God has an inheritance. This inheritance is in His Son, Jesus Christ. This means that
all of the hope, vision, expectation, and goals of the Father are (and
have been) accomplished in and by His Son. The Father has invested
everything in His Son. In human terms, you could say that God has
been "saving up" and "investing" in His only Son since before eternity. This means that all of the works of God have been done in, by, and
for the Son. All of God's creation (visible and invisible) is not only an
expression of but also an investment into His Son.

But it's not only His works. What about His character? Yes, all
of God's love, mercy, kindness, truth, long-suffering, grace, wisdom,

and forgiveness are invested into His Son, as well as His righteousness, justice, and judgment. *All* of His character.

But it's not only His works and character. What about His power? All of His supernatural power is also invested into His Son. Miracles, healing, and resurrection are also included. You see, the Father really has invested His everything into His Son. There is no inheritance that has more fullness than this one. All other inheritances are but shadows of this one true and real inheritance.

He really is the heir of all things!

"But those vine-growers said to one another, 'This is the heir; come, let us kill him, and the *inheritance* will be ours!'" (Mark 12:7). The Son has an inheritance given to Him by His Father.

"...to open their eyes so that they may turn from darkness to light and from the dominion of Satan to God, that they may receive forgiveness of sins and an *inheritance* among those who have been sanctified by faith in Me" (Acts 26:18). The sons of God have an inheritance given to them by the Son.

"...also we have obtained an *inheritance*, having been predestined according to His purpose who works all things after the counsel of His will" (Eph. 1:11). Who are the "we" referred to here? The "we" is the ekklesia.

"I pray that the eyes of your heart may be enlightened, so that you will know what is the hope of His calling, what are the riches of the glory of *His inheritance* in the saints" (Ephesians 1:18) . It's clear from this passage (and others) that Christ has an inheritance. But where is His inheritance? Ah! His inheritance is in the saints.

But where is the inheritance of the saints? "...knowing that from the Lord you will receive the reward of the inheritance. It is the Lord Christ whom you serve" (Col. 3:24). The Lord Christ Himself is the inheritance of the saints. So, He is our inheritance and we are His inheritance. How is this possible? It's possible because of a little word called "in." Christ is *in* us and we are *in* Him!

So, considering all that I have said about this inheritance of God and all that He has invested into His Son, now ponder this: The heir of all things is *our* inheritance! And this heir lives inside of us! He is our life! He is our food! He is our drink! He is our everything!

The Sole Expression of the Glory of God

Jesus Christ our Lord is the only perfectly full expression of God. You could say that God (the Father, Son, and Holy Spirit) only has one declaration, representation, utterance, manifestation, and expression and that is His Son.

God, who is invisible, wanted to have a visible expression or manifestation of Himself. He wanted to be expressed in all realms—visible and invisible. Since He is Spirit (John 4:24), this means that He is invisible to the natural (physical) eye. This is why He created man (Gen. 1:26-28). The whole story of the creation is a picture or shadow of our wonderful Lord Jesus Christ!

The Spiritual Reality of the Physical Creation

As I have said, all of the scriptures speak of Jesus Christ: "You search the scriptures because you suppose that in them you have eternal life. It is these that testify about Me" (John 5:39). This means that the creation story in Genesis is actually a picture or shadow of Jesus Christ. Let's take a brief look at this story through the lens of Christ.

"In the beginning God created the heavens and the earth..." (Gen. 1:1). Even though Christ is not a created being (He is "uncreated"), He is a being of the heavenly nature *and* the earthly nature. He is both God and man. He is a being of the heavens and the earth.

And then there is the light. "Then God said, 'Let there be light' and there was light…" (Gen. 1:3). "Jesus spoke to the people once more and said, 'I am the light of the world. If you follow Me, you won't have to walk in darkness, because you will have the light that leads to life'" (John 8:12). "And God said, Let there be lights in the expanse of the heavens to divide between the day and the night. And let them be for signs, and for seasons, and for days and years" (Gen. 1:14). "In Him was life, and the life was the light of men. And the light shines in the darkness, and the darkness did not overtake it" (John 1:4-5). Christ is the true light from the Father and the only way to the Father. He is the light (or expression) of the invisible God.

"God called the light 'day,' and the darkness He called 'night.' So there was evening and there was morning—one day" (Gen 1:5). Have you ever considered your dear Lord as your *new day*? He is your new dawn, your fresh start, your "reboot" on life! Whenever you are dragging throughout your day all you need to do is turn to Him and you immediately get a new day. Wow! What a Christ! He is our new day. (See the author's book *New Day* for further reading on this subject.)

> God called the expanse "sky." So there was evening and there was morning—a second day. Then God said, "Let the water below the sky be gathered to one place. Let the dry ground appear." And it happened so. God called the dry ground "land," and the collection of the water He called "seas." And God saw that it was good (Gen. 9-10).

Now we can see that He is our evening and our morning. We can see that He is our sky (heaven) and our earth. He is also our ground that rose up out of the water. On the third day He rose up out of the "death waters" and provided a refuge of life for us—resurrected life. Life that has conquered death and decay and destruction.

> Then God said, "Let the land sprout grass, green plants yield-ing seed, fruit trees making fruit, each according to its species with seed in it, upon the land." And it happened so. The land brought forth grass, green plants yielding seed, each accord-ing to its species, and trees making fruit with the seed in it, each according to its species. And God saw that it was good (Gen. 11:12).

Incredible! Now we see that on the foundation of the earth that rose up out of the death waters there is now life! There are seeds that contains abundant life. And the life that these seeds contain is eternal and reproduces and multiplies an abundant harvest! Brothers and sis-ters, is Christ your seed? "Truly, truly, I say to you, unless a grain of wheat falls into the ground and dies, it abides alone; but if it dies, it brings forth much fruit" (John 12:24).

There are three very important points seen here. First, in Him is life. The reason that God's life is in the Son is that *He is* the life! How could eternal life be anywhere else but inside of the One who is life itself?

Secondly, this very same life is the light of men. Did you get that? Life is light! Remember, we are talking about God's life here—eternal, everlasting, spiritual life. Nothing can stop this life. Nothing can dete-riorate this life. Time and space cannot wear down this life in the least. In fact, this life is outside of time and space! This life has seen and gone through death and come out the other side brighter than before. This life has conquered death. Death cannot touch it. The world system cannot effect this life at all. This life has also overcome the world! This life has also overcome satan and all his cohorts. This life is the light and brings revelation and exposure of the darkness where ever it goes. Notice that if you enter a pitch-dark room and then turn on the light, all of the darkness must flee. The light not only exposes the darkness, it also causes the darkness to run away completely.

And thirdly...this life lives inside of you! (See the author's book *The Temple Within*.)

The life brings light and the light brings life. God created light first. Then He created life. You cannot have life without light. After He created light then there was life. Also, the more light He created, the more life He could then create. Light brings life. That is a spiritual principle. Before there can be any spiritual life in you there must be spiritual light (or revelation). The more revelation you have, the more life you will have.

> And God said, "Let Us make man in Our image, after Our likeness. And let them have dominion over the fish of the sea, and over the fowl of the heavens, and over the cattle, and over all the earth, and over all the creepers creeping on the earth." And God created man in His image; in the image of God He created him. He created them male and female (Gen. 1:26-27).

Now here again we can see the eternal purpose of God emerging in the text. Why did God create mankind? It was for Him to have an image. Another way to put it, He wanted an expression of Himself. He wanted to have a display of Himself in the visible realm. He wanted to have a physical, visible likeness of His nature, His character, His attributes, His mind, and His heart. God, who is spirit, wanted to have a visible representation of His invisible person. This is the reason for His creation of mankind. There is no other reason—but oh, what a glorious reason!

It's hard for me to phathom that God would do such a thing. Just think: He created us—that is, all of mankind—to be His image, reflection, expression, manifestation, and representation of all that He is! Wow! What a God! What a purpose! I simply cannot imagine any higher purpose than that.

Then God placed His new creation (mankind) into a garden. That really tells us something about God's original purpose for mankind. He wanted mankind to live and work in a garden. He wanted mankind to be "of the earth." The text also says that God planted a garden: "And Jehovah God planted a garden in Eden, at the east, and He set there the man whom He had formed" (Gen. 2:8). God wanted mankind to take care of the earth. Not only that, but mankind himself was made out of the dust of the earth: "Then the LORD God took some soil from the ground and formed a man out of it; He breathed life-giving breath into his nostrils and the man began to live" (Gen. 2:7).

God created a race of "earth beings" who were created out of the earth and for the earth. Of course, this was totally in line with His eternal purpose of having a visible representation of Himself, a spiritual being.

The narrative in these chapters in Genesis is a direct physical reflection of spiritual realities revealed to us in John's letter of the Revelation. This is an extremely import matter to see with your spiritual eyes! The first two books of the Bible directly relate (in picture form) to the last two books of the Bible (in spiritual form). Genesis chapters one and two give to us an illustration (or picture) of God's intention or desire and reason for creating.

If you pay close attention while you are reading Genesis chapters one and two you will find several items displayed for us. In chapter one He created the universe, including light, darkness, day, night, water, sky, evening, morning, earth, sea, plants, birds, fish, animals.

Now, in chapter two, God gets more specific concerning His eternal purpose in relation to mankind himself and the purpose for mankind. God describes the garden in more detail. He tells Adam about his diet: He can eat from any of the fruit bearing trees (including the Tree of Life) but cannot eat of the tree of the knowledge of good and evil. Isn't this amazing?

What is striking to me here is what God *doesn't* do. God doesn't give mankind a set of do's and don'ts. He doesn't give him a "mission" or "ministry." He doesn't give man any lessons in theology or doctrine. God doesn't give mankind a master plan for his life. He doesn't even explain to mankind why He created or what He is going to do with this creation now that it exists. Instead, God seems to be interested and concerned with only one thing pertaining to man: His diet!

Have you ever thought about that? The main concern God had for Adam was his diet: what he ate and what he didn't eat. That, my friends, is still the most important thing on the heart of God for mankind. Remember the saying that "you are what you eat?" I'm not referring to physical food here. This is not a plea to eat healthy foods! Though I do believe in that, I am referring to spiritual food. The *true* food. The *true* riches. What kind of food are you eating, dear reader? (We will explore this fact in much more depth in the next part of this book. Suffice it to say for now that most Christians are sorely lacking in revelation and spiritual practice in this matter.)

Then God did something even more amazing. He created for Adam a help meet by opening his side and taking her out of him. He put Adam asleep, opened his side, and proceeded to remove another person from inside of Adam. Does this sound familiar to you at all? Perhaps quoting a few scriptural references for you will help.

> And so wives must submit themselves completely to their husbands just as the church submits itself to Christ. Husbands, love your wives just as Christ loved the church and gave His life for it. He did this to dedicate the church to God by His word, after making it clean by washing it in water, in order to present the church to Himself in all its beauty—pure and faultless, without spot or wrinkle or any other imperfection (Eph. 5:24-27).

> But when they came to Jesus, they saw that He was already dead, so they did not break His legs. One of the soldiers, however, plunged his spear into Jesus' side, and at once blood and water poured out (John 19:33-34).

Here in Ephesians and the gospel of John we see a very clear reference to what happened in the garden when God opened Adam's side. That whole story is very clearly a "picture" or "foreshadow" of Christ and the church! And to make it even clearer, Paul refers to Christ as the "second Adam."

> For just as all people die because of their union with Adam, in the same way all will be raised to life because of their union with Christ (1 Cor. 15:22).

> For the scripture says, the first man, Adam, was created a living being but the last Adam is the life-giving Spirit. The first Adam, made of earth, came from the earth; the second Adam came from heaven (1 Cor. 15:45-47).

So here it is, my friends, the eternal purpose of God described for us in detail in Genesis chapters one through three. And, of course, there is much more to it than that. We can never arrive at the end of describing this awesome and glorious Christ.

Chapter Five

The Christ Who is All

...and having put on the new, which is renewed in regard to knowledge, after the image of Him who did create him; where there is not Greek and Jew, circumcision and uncircumcision, foreigner, Scythian, servant, freeman—but the all and in all—Christ (Col. 3:10, 11).

But when all things are subjected to Him, then the Son Himself also will be subject to Him who has subjected all things to Him, so that God may be all things in all (1 Cor. 15:28).

...because in him were all things created, those in the heavens, and those upon the earth, those visible, and those invisible, whether thrones, whether lordships, whether principalities, whether authorities; all things through him, and for him, have been created,and himself is before all, and the all things in him have consisted (Col. 1:16, 17).

...which He wrought in the Christ, having raised him out of the dead, and did set him at His right hand in the heavenly plac-es, far above all principality, and authority, and might, and lordship, and every name named, not only in this age, but also in the coming one; and all things He did put under his feet, and did give him—head over all things to the assembly, which is his body, the fulness of Him who is filling the all in all (Eph. 1:20-23).

Remember that in God's eye there is only Christ, not things. He sees neither affairs nor things, He only beholds Christ. The affairs and things which we usually think of are non-existent in the view of God. (Christ: *The Sum of All Spiritual Things* by Watchman Nee)

The Fulfillment of God's Purpose

As we can see from the verses above (and others), the intention of the eternal purpose is that all things would find their fulfillment in Christ: That He would be the all in all. Of course, He is already the all of God. The Father has placed all of His fullness into Christ through the Holy Spirit. As we have already seen, since Christ is the inheritance of God, He is the all of God. All of God's desires, dreams, vision, intentions, purposes, and hopes have already been fulfilled in and through His Son. You could say that God has invested everything He is and has into His Son. This has all been accomplished through the Holy Spirit. But as wonderful as this is, God still wants more.

The All in All

In order for God to get His expression in His people, His Son must become the all in all. This means that Christ must become the *all*, that is, the *everything*, in all of His people. He already is the all of God. But now, to get His expression in this realm, He must become the *all* in all of the members of His Body. Are you seeing this? Are you getting it? The <u>all</u> (Christ) in <u>all</u> (the members of His body).

Most believers have not seen or taken Christ as their All. To these believers Christ is a *giver of things* (such as salvation, redemption, provision)—He is not the things themselves (the savior, the redeemer, the provider). He is not their all, their everything. There is a huge difference!

Chances are that you, dear reader, are one of those believers. You have never really *seen* or *applied* Christ as your all. You have never really seen Christ as the sum of all spiritual things. *Seeing* Christ as your all is the first step. The next step is *applying* that revelation into your daily life and circumstances. This book has been written to help you with both of these areas. This section which we are currently in is to help you with the *seeing* aspect. If you cannot see, then you cannot apply. Dear reader, you will need to pursuit your Lord for this seeing. You will need to ask Him to show you these things. Reading a book can help, but it will never bring you to the place of seeing and experiencing His reality. You must go directly to Him for that.

He is a Person

> He is also head of the body, the church; and He is the beginning, the firstborn from the dead, so that He Himself will come to have first place in everything (Col. 1:18).

This person has a head and a body, like all true persons. But notice with me in this verse from Colossians 1 that this very important phrase is employed: *so that He Himself*. Whenever you see the word "so" or "so that" or "that" it means that the writer is now giving the reason for everything he said before it. The "so that" is the purpose behind the previous statement. So here, Paul is now giving us the reason or purpose for Him being the head of the body, the beginning, and the firstborn from the dead. It's all so that He Himself will come to have the first place in everything. Could Paul get more emphatic than this? Why didn't he just say "so that He will come to have the first place in everything?" Why this *He Himself* business? Obviously, Paul was emphasizing something here. Part of that is the awesome fact that our Christ is a living person. To me, *He Himself* strongly denotes personhood. Jesus Christ is a person. Yes, He is divine, which means that God is a person. But He is also a human person. He is personhood in all of its fullness. Both human and divine. All personhood comes from Him. And that is wonderful, but I would like to touch upon something else relating to *He Himself*.

I see this phrase not only as a reference to his personhood but also as a bold declaration of this glorious person being the all in all. You see, He is the all in all not just because He is a divine and human person but also because of who He is! This is a very difficult idea to understand with our minds—it can only be spiritually discerned. But let me try to communicate it to you and pray that God will give revelation.

Seeing that *He Himself* is our only person means that we now have no other personhood within ourselves but Christ. "I have been crucified with Christ; and it is no longer I who live, but Christ lives in me..." (Gal. 2:20a). What a declaration Paul makes here! He is saying that the person of Christ is now his all, his everything. There is no Paul left...only Christ.

Dear believer, do you realize that there is no more of *you* left? That Christ is your all? That this wonderful person has now taken residence inside of you and really, spiritually, as far as God is concerned, there is only Christ? When the Father beholds you, He only sees His beautifully wonderful Son. That's exactly what Paul is declaring to us in Colossians. And that is very exciting and wonderful and glorious. But there is also another point I want to make here.

Crucified with Christ

If Christ is now our only life (and He definitely is), then how can we now view Him from the lens of our own selfish desires (our wants and needs)? A person who is dead no longer has any self-interests or viewpoints. A dead person (in Christ) only has one viewpoint: Christ Himself!

He doesn't see Christ as a means to an end. As I like to say, he doesn't see Christ as his "ER" person. Of course, we normally think of the phrase "ER" as referring to the emergency room in a hospital. That's where we go when we have an emergency in our lives. And this is how we treat Christ: as our "ER" person.

He is our:

HelpER	LeadER
ProvidER	BackER
HealER	WorkER
GivER	GofER
PartnER	BaptizER

This list betrays a certain mindset. All of these things point to the believer himself...not to Christ Himself. All of these things are about what Christ can do for the believer. Can you understand that seeing

Christ from these viewpoints is not seeing *He Himself* but is instead beholding *you, yourself*? You are seeing Christ from the perspective of what He can do for you, not for who He is. *You* are still at the center. You are still the focal point. *You* are relating to your Christ from within the filter of your own self-interests.

If this is you, believe me, you are not alone. We have all fallen into that trap.

But what if...

You could break free from all that "self" and really learn to see your Lord as He is, as the *all*?

What if...

The power of the veil of flesh was already broken by Christ on the cross and you could actually see Him and know Him without the veil or hindrance of your own self-interests?

What if...

This Christ could be seen and known by you just as you are known by Him?

Well keep reading, dear saints, because that's exactly what we will be covering in the coming pages of this book.

Christ as Our Canaan Land

One of the most full and beautiful pictures of Christ that we have in all of scripture is that of the Canaan land. Paul sets the precedence for this in the first chapter to the Colossians: "...giving thanks to the Father, who has made us fit for a share of the inheritance of the saints in light" (Col. 1:12).

The literal translation of the word "inheritance" in the verse above is the *allotted portion*. This is a direct reference made by Paul to the Canaan land of Israel. If you will recall, as they entered the land

God divided it up according to portions. Each tribe received their allotted portion, which, of course, totaled twelve portions.

What was Paul strongly implying with this comparison? I think that it's actually quite clear. Paul is saying to us that Christ is our Canaan land. Every believer has been given a portion of this Christ in whom we can live, breathe, and move. In this Christ there are unlimited supplies of His immeasurable riches.

Can we live off of this land? Absolutely! Let's take a look at this description of the Canaan land from Deuteronomy and find all of the ways we can live off this land.

> ...because the LORD your God is bringing you to a good land—a land with rivers and deep springs flowing to the valleys and hills. It's a land filled with wheat, barley, vines, fig trees, and pomegranates. It's a land filled with olive oil and honey—a land without scarcity. You'll eat food in it and lack nothing. It's a land where its rocks are iron and you can dig copper from its mountains (Deut. 8:7-9).

A Land of Rivers and Deep Springs Flowing

> Jesus answered her, "Everyone who drinks this water will become thirsty again. But whoever drinks the water that I will give him will never become thirsty again. The water that I will give him will become a well of water for him, springing up to eternal life" (John 4:13, 14).

> On the last and most important day of the festival, Jesus stood up and shouted, "If anyone is thirsty, let him come to me and

drink! The one who believes in me, as the scripture has said, will have rivers of living water flowing from his heart" (John 7:37, 38).

The Lord clearly tells us here that His Spirit, His life, is the *true* water. The physical water that we see in rivers and springs or drink everyday is just a shadow or picture of the *true* water, who is Christ. Just think about this for a moment. He tells us that not only is He the real water but that if we drink of this water we will never be thirsty again. But that's not all...if we drink this water, there will form within us a *well of water* that will spring up eternally. Wow! Not only can we drink of Him at any time but the endless water supply is actually *within us*. My dear saints, it just doesn't get any better than this!

A Land with an Endless Supply of Water

This water represents the life and spirit of Christ Himself. We can see that this water is both alive and flowing because it is represented by both rivers and springs. Both of these are constantly moving, which speaks of life. Not only that, but these sources of life flow in both the valleys and the hills. In other words...everywhere! It doesn't matter if you are currently having a "mountain-top" experience or if you are down in the "dumps" of the valley. The living water is there for you to drink in every place and in every situation. What a Lord!

A Land Filled with Wheat and Barley

Truly, I tell all of you with certainty, unless a grain of wheat falls into the ground and dies, it remains alone. But if it dies, it produces a lot of grain (John 12:24).

First of all, in John 12:24, the Lord tells us that He is the grain of wheat that falls into the ground and dies. Of course, this one grain produced many grains through His resurrection. The many grains are us, the church. Secondly, the barley is the first crop to come up out of the ground. Our Lord is the *first fruits*, that is, the first one to be resurrected. We all follow Him in that resurrection.

The life of Christ *is* resurrection life. It is divine life that has conquered death—that is, death in all its forms. Please don't just think of this in physical terms. Yes, Jesus Christ physically rose from the dead and conquered death of the body. But what about death of the soul? What about death of the mind and heart? What about death of a vision? Have you ever noticed that when God gives you a vision for something He will also bring it into death? I have seen this many times in my own life and ministry. He gives me a vision—something that I know is from Him and for Him. And yet He usually doesn't fulfill that vision right away. First, it has to go into a "death mode." At the beginning it is very alive and real and exciting. But then it begins to fade as time goes by. At that point, I usually begin to wonder (and perhaps even doubt) if it was from God in the first place. But if it is from the Lord, it will remain somewhere deep within our spirits. It's kind of like sleeping. The Bible refers to death as sleeping many times. The vision isn't totally gone, but it has definitely now faded into the background in our hearts and minds. It is asleep. This is death of a vision.

We need to understand that this "death stage" is very important for us. During this stage we learn to "let go and let God," so to speak. We can become very possessive of our visions and think that they are something that we own. But they are not! They belong totally to God. If we take them as our own, then He will wait (during the death stage) for us to give them back to Him with our hearts. When this happens then there will be a breaking that takes place inside of us that is vitally important for our transformation into His life. That is, His resurrection life.

This life/death/life process will take place many times in the life of a believer. Those who learn to lay down their lives on a continuous basis will experience and display His resurrection life. Those lives will express His life and that expression will bear much fruit in the lives of many other saints.

A Land with Vines, Fig Trees, and Pomegranates

> I am the true vine, and My Father is the gardener. Every branch in Me that does not bear fruit, He takes away; and every branch that bears fruit, He trims so that it may bear more fruit. You are already clean because of the word I have spoken to you. Abide in Me, and I will abide in you. The branch cannot itself produce fruit, unless it abides on the vine. Likewise, you cannot produce fruit unless you abide in Me (John 15:1-4).

> Seeing a lone fig tree by the road, He came up to it and found
> nothing on it except leaves only. And He said to it, "May no fruit
> ever come from you again!" And the fig tree shriveled up at
> once (Matt. 21:19).

> Your shoots are an orchard of pomegranates with choice fruit,
> henna with nard... (Song of Songs 4:13).

In all of these passages we see one common denominator...life! The Lord's goal with the church is to have the results or expression of His life. That's fruit. In the case of all three of these examples, the goal is fruit but the means (or method) is life. If there is no life flowing in the vine then you will have no grapes. If there is no life flowing in the fig tree then you will have no figs. If there is no life flowing in the pomegranate tree then you will not have even one pomegranate. The tree will be dry, fruitless, and ugly.

The pomegranate is particularly interesting to me. Paintings and illustrations of the fruit were placed all over the inside of the tabernacle and temple, including rows and rows of pomegranate trees painted on the walls of the temple.

And have you ever cut a pomegranate open? What do you get? Loads of seeds! Can you imagine how many seeds are in a grove of pomegranate trees? Probably millions. But now let's take it a step further. Each individual seed has the potential to produce many more trees and thus, many more seeds. And on and on it goes. Of course, this speaks of abundant life. His life isn't just great and wonderful and beautiful. It is abundant! It is without end. It is incredibly full and rich and has no limits or borders. "The thief does not come except that he may steal, and kill, and destroy. I came that they may have life and may have it abundantly" (John 10:10).

But that's not all...

All of that abundant life is contained within the temple—that is, the house of the living God. You see, God wants all of His abundant, eternal, everlasting life to be seen, experienced, and expressed from within His house. That's the church!

A Land Filled with Olive Oil and Honey

> And going out, according to His custom, He went to the Mount of Olives; and His disciples also followed Him. And having come on the place, He said to them, "Pray that you do not enter into temptation." And He was withdrawn from them, about a stone's throw. And having placed the knees, He prayed, saying, "Father, if You purpose it, take away this cup from Me; but not My will be done, but let Yours be done" (Luke 22:39-42).

It is no coincidence that your Lord went to the Mount of Olive to wrestle with His Father in prayer concerning His own death. Do you know how olive oil is produced? By pressing or crushing the olives. This was the Lord's time of crushing and being pressed by the will of His Father for completing His mission. This whole incident drips with the fragrance of death by crucifixion. This is all about the cross. Not just the Lord going to the cross for our salvation, but also for the *life of the cross*. The actual act of Christ going to the cross was the apex of a life lived by that cross. He lived a life in submission to the will of His Father. In fact, He told us that it was not even His own life—that He did the works of the Father. He spoke the words of the Father. He lived by the life of His Father. And then He told us to live by His own life...not our own! "Then Jesus said to His disciples, 'If anyone desires to come after Me, let him deny himself, and let him bear his cross, and let him follow Me'" (Matt. 16:24).

Saints, the honey is found in the body of a lion. The sweet, sweet food of life is found within the Lord's own body. He is the Lion of the tribe of Judah and the honey is only to be found in His body.

The whole process of bees making honey is an incredibly beautiful picture of Christ and the church. It all begins with the worker bees. There are three kinds of bees in the hive: the queens, the young workers, and the mature workers. The mature worker bees are the ones that go out into the world to find nectar. Of course, they find it in various plants and flowers. They are equipped with a special sack inside their bodies to hold this nectar. Once they are full of nectar they return to the hive. There, they connect with the younger worker bees and then they suck nectar out of foragers' honey sacs and mix it—in their stomachs—with a naturally occurring enzyme called invertase that breaks the nectar's sucrose down into glucose and fructose. After workers convert the sugars they regurgitate the transformed nectar into the outer cells of the hive, then fan it with their wings to drive away moisture. The honey is then sealed with a wax cap to be tapped for food during the long winter months.

Wow! What a wonderful shadow of the reality of Christ and His body. The saints go out into the world to find the "nectar," which is the sweet life of Christ Himself. They store it in a special "compartment" inside of them called *their* spirit. Then, they bring it back to the hive and share it with the other bees, or their community. Life is shared and all are fed. The nectar (life) is also stored within the hive as a reserve to share with the saints and others in the world.

And this all takes place within the body of a *lion*!

(If the church life that I just described above is totally foreign to you then please do not despair. It is God's will for you, too, dear believer. There is help available. I will be referring to the "hive life" of bees [believers] throughout this book. If this sparks something inside of you and you would like more information, then please contact us. Our contact information is located at the back of this book.)

A Land Where Rocks Are Iron and its Mountains Have Copper

And Moses and Aaron assembled the congregation before the rock. And he said to them, Hear now, you rebels, shall we bring forth water to you out of this rock? And Moses lifted up his hand and smote the rock with his rod twice; and much water came out; and the congregation and their animals drank (Num. 20:10, 11).

And all were baptized to Moses in the cloud, and in the Sea, and all ate the same spiritual food. And all drank the same spiritual drink; for they drank of the spiritual rock following, and that Rock was Christ (1 Cor. 10:2-4).

For you have not drawn near to the mountain being touched, and having been lit with fire, and to gloom, and darkness, and tempest, and to a sound of trumpet, and to a voice of words, which those hearing begged that not a word be added to them; for they could not bear the thing enjoined: "Even if a beast touches the mountain, it will be stoned, or shot through with a dart." And so fearful was the thing appearing, Moses said, "I am terrified and trembling." But you have drawn near Mount Zion, even the city of the living God, to a heavenly Jerusalem, and to myriads of angels, and to a gathering, an assembly of the first-born ones having been enrolled in Heaven; and to God the Judge of all, and to spirits of just ones who have been perfected; and to Jesus the Mediator of a new covenant, and to blood of sprinkling speaking better things than of Abel (Heb. 12:18-24).

It is out of the rocks and mountains that we dig our most precious minerals. We know that Christ alone is our true rock and out from Him alone do we find the riches of the living God. But it takes some digging. It takes some *mining* to unravel His character, nature, power, and life. This is the importance and glory of beholding our wonderful Lord. There is nothing like face-to-face communion with Him.

Once, my wife and I and some friends went to visit Australia to share our precious Lord with some believers in the cities of Perth and Melbourne (Ballarat). While in Ballarat, we visited some of the old gold mines left from their gold rush in the 1850s. We actually went on a tour down underground into the mines to see what the miners experienced when they dug for gold. It was dark and cold, the air was thin, and sometimes there would be a collapse of the caves and many would die. It was definitely not a pleasant situation! I was absolutely amazed by how much these men had sacrificed with the hopes of striking it rich. Basically, they sacrificed their very lives in the hopes of finding some gold. Most of them never did. Many families up on the surface lost sons, husbands, fathers, and brothers. And for what? Some rocks that had some shiny metal inside?

While I was listening to this story being told by the tour guide I realized something: People will do all kinds of crazy things to make it rich. They will even risk their lives to *hit the big one*. They will travel all over the world, go to extreme risk and expense to find some hope of making the big time and striking it rich.

But how many will sacrifice their lives for the true riches?

> This grace was given to me, I being less than the least of all the saints, to preach the gospel of the unsearchable riches of Christ among the nations, and to bring to light all, what is the fellowship of the mystery having been hidden from eternity in God, the One creating all things through Jesus Christ (Eph 3:8, 9).

Brothers and sisters, I can tell you without any doubt that this "mining" for the true riches of Christ will cost you. What will it cost, you may ask? Maybe time? Money? Effort? Family? Convenience? Leisure? No, not at all. It will not cost you any of those things. It will only cost you one thing.

Your life!

> And He said to all, If anyone desires to come after Me, let him deny himself and take up his cross daily. And let him follow Me. For whoever desires to save his life, he will lose it. But whoever loses his life for My sake, this one will save it (Luke 9:23, 24).

PART TWO

Learning to See this Christ

*"You can't stop us on the road to freedom, you can't stop us
cuz our eyes can see"*
Van Morrison – Topelo Honey

"Behold now the kingdom... see with new eyes"
John Michael Talbot – The Painter

*"With an open heaven you see, and you see
God's meaning concerning His Son"*
T. Austin-Sparks

*"But we all with our face having been unveiled, having beheld the
glory of the Lord in a mirror, are being changed into the same image
from glory to glory, as from the Lord Spirit."*
2 Cor. 3:16

Chapter Six

The Importance of Spiritual Sight

Then Jesus answered and said to them, Truly, truly, I say to you, The Son is not able to do anything from Himself, except what He may see the Father doing; for whatever that One does, these things also the Son does likewise (John 5:19).

Notice that Jesus said (several times) that He could not do anything unless He first saw the Father do it. This gives us an incredible insight into how the Son of God functioned while on the earth. Of course, hearing was also extremely important element in their relationship as we can see further down in this passage in verses twenty-four and twenty-five. However, for the sake of this writing, I will focus on the function of seeing. I believe that this aspect of knowing the Lord deeply has been largely ignored by the Christian community at large for centuries. Most Christians know little (if not practically nothing) concerning spiritual sight. Most Bible teaching, preaching, and writing focuses on the faculty of "hearing the Lord" instead of "seeing the Lord." This, I believe, has meant great loss for the church at large. Jesus saw the Father doing things, and then simply "copied" what He saw the Father do.

Christians seem to hear all kinds of things from God. Some may actually be hearing the Lord (and some are definitely not!). But why is this? Why do we hear things that are not God speaking to us? Along with having Christ living in us we also have our own minds, wills, and emotions. More times than not we are simply hearing our own thoughts or feelings or wills. Sometimes it may even be satanic influence. This is a huge road block to us hearing and knowing the Lord in an intimate way.

Now some of you may be thinking that this is where the Bible comes in: We simply need to know the scriptures and do what they say. Now I strongly believe in the veracity of the scriptures. It is the God-breathed and God-inspired written word of God.

However, notice with me please that the scripture quoted above in John 5:19 tells us that Jesus only did the things which He saw the Father do. He also said elsewhere that He only spoke the words that the Father spoke. Notice the Lord's point of reference for all things that He did and spoke on the earth was a *person*. It was because of His *relationship with His Father* that He knew what to do and what to say.

"And the Father who sent me, He has given testimony concerning me. None of you have ever either heard His voice or seen what He is like" (John 5:37). There it is. None of you have ever either heard His voice or *seen* what He is like.

I would like to point out two things about this relationship between the Father and the Son through the Spirit that we see so beautifully portrayed in the earthly life of Christ. First of all, in order to hear and see what another person is doing, you have to get close to them. Of course, we know that the Father and the Son are so close that they are one. That's what I call closeness!

They had always been one in spirit throughout all of eternity. But now, something had changed. The Son became a human. In a sense, He became limited by His flesh—you could say that there was a "veil" of flesh between Him and the Father. He was on the earth and there were many things happening all around Him that were not really good things. It would have been very easy for Him to be distracted by those things, people, and events. He had to learn to hear and see the Father in new ways. At times, He actually needed to get away from it all and spend some quality time with the Father alone. This meant a deliberate movement of His will towards the Father. In other words, He had to learn how to fellowship with God as a human. He showed us the way by becoming the way.

Secondly, the Lord Jesus was extremely active in ministering to others. He always kept his eyes on the Father and was therefore led by the Spirit as to where to go and who to speak to. The source of His "leading" was not just the scriptures. There is no indication whatsoever that He read the "Bible verse for the day" and then did what it said. No, that's not the life He lived by.

And here is my point: **He had to keep his eyes on the Father at all times**. Keeping his eyes fixed upon the Father gave Him the ability to "hear" the Father.

As I have said, Christians talk and write a lot about "hearing" but very few are sharing about "seeing." And I believe that this is why there is so little hearing the Lord: Seeing must precede hearing.

Seeing Must Precede Hearing

Your spiritual hearing will definitely be impaired if you haven't learned to spiritually see. Jesus could hear God speaking to Him (as a man) because He continually had His eyes fixed on the Father. You see, the fact that Christ was always looking at His Father opened the door for Him to hear. Let me use a very physical illustration for this. Let's say that you are going to have a conversation with another person. Would you turn your back to that person before your conversation? If you did, you would no doubt misunderstand many of the words they were speaking. Besides it being incredibly rude, as they spoke you would not be able to see their mouth move, the expressions on their face, and so on. Hearing another person speak requires your full attention. And this means focus. Not only the focus of your eyes, but also the focus of your heart and mind.

Jesus was continually turning His mind, will, and emotions toward the Father. He was always focusing all of His attention on the God who lived inside of Him. So much so that whenever the Father spoke, Jesus instantly knew what He wanted. Why? Because His only focus was the Father! You could say that He had a "holy obsession" with His Father. His eye was single. This singular focus kept the channel open for communication and the ability to hear His Father in whatever circumstances He was in at the time. This was the secret of His power and life as a man. And He told us this over and over again: "Even as the living Father sent Me, and I live through the Father; also the one partaking Me, even that one will live through Me" (John 6:57).

Turn Your Attention Upon Jesus

I'm sure that most of you, if not all, have heard the famous old song: "Turn Your Eyes Upon Jesus." But what you may not know is how this wonderful song came about. "The Heavenly Vision" (also known as "Turn Your Eyes Upon Jesus" from the first line of its chorus), is a hymn written by Helen Howarth Lemmel. It was inspired by a tract entitled *Focused* written by the missionary Isabella Lilias Trotter. Lilias Trotter wrote and painted much about focusing on Christ alone and I highly recommend her writings and artwork.

Turn your eyes upon Jesus
Look full in His wonderful face
And the things of earth will grow strangely dim
In the light of His glory and grace

Turning your eyes upon Jesus means to turn your attention to only Him. *To look full in His wonderful face* means that no other object will distract you from full attention, full focus, and full engagement with your glorious Lord.

That sounds wonderful, doesn't it? But how do you get there? How do you learn to lay aside all of the distractions of this world system, the things you see around you, and the thoughts and feelings of your own mind and heart? First, we must see the importance of this. Then we must learn to put away those things which would hinder us from seeing and abiding with this wonderful Christ who lives within us.

The lamp of the body is the eye. When your eyesight is good, your whole body also is lighted up; but when it is defective, your body is darkened (Luke 11:34).

I advise you to buy from Me gold having been fired by fire, that you may be rich; and white garments, that you may be clothed,

and your shame and nakedness may not be revealed. And
anoint your eyes with eye salve, that you may see (Rev. 3:18).

...that the God of our Lord Jesus Christ, the Father of glory,
may give unto you a spirit of wisdom and revelation in the
knowledge of Him; having the eyes of your heart enlightened,
that ye may know what is the hope of His calling, what the riches of the glory of His inheritance in the saints (Eph. 1:17-18).

...to open their eyes, that they may turn from darkness to light
and from the power of Satan unto God, that they may receive
remission of sins and an inheritance among them that are sanctified by faith in Me (Acts 26:18).

A high value is placed upon spiritual sight in the scriptures. But
have we contemplated the immense lack of spiritual sight and the
gross spiritual blindness that is in our lives? Before we can begin to
look and really "see" the Lord in a spiritual way, we must first examine
why we have such a hindrance to this sight. Spiritual blindness is the
reason, but what are the causes for the blindness?

In *The Candlestick of All Gold*, T. Austin-Sparks explains, "In the
Revelation this is 'He that hath an ear, let Him hear,' and in the case
of Laodicea—which represents the end—it is 'I counsel thee to buy of
me eyesalve that thou mayest see.' 'And I turned to see the voice that
spake with me,' said John. God is speaking, He has something to say,
but there must be 'a Spirit of wisdom and revelation in the knowledge
of Him, the eyes of your heart being enlightened.'"

The problem is that most believer's spiritual eyesight is what I
would call *fuzzy*. You could say that the problem is *spiritual cataracts*.
When you have physical cataracts there is a fog or haze over the lenses

of your eyes. You can see, but not clearly. As the cataracts progress, the haze progresses and eventually you cannot even drive a vehicle safely. But the faculty of our spiritual sight is not located in our heads or in our minds, emotions, or wills. In the next chapter, we will explore spiritual sight.

Chapter Seven

The Causes of Spiritual Blindness

Then having such hope, we use much boldness. And not as Moses, who put a veil over his face, for the sons of Israel not to gaze at the end of the thing being done away. But their thoughts were hardened, for until the present time the same veil remains on the reading of the Old Covenant, not being unveiled, that it is being done away in Christ. But until today, when Moses is being read, a veil lies on their heart. But whenever it turns to the Lord, the veil is taken away (2 Cor. 3:12-16).

Saul of Tarsus was definitely a person who could speak about blindness and sight. When he was on the road to Damascus he was about as spiritually blind as anyone could be. He was blinded by his own religious zeal. He was blinded by his zeal for God, his zeal for tradition, and his zeal for the Jewish religion. He was blinded way before God supernaturally removed his natural eyesight on the road that day. By God removing his physical sight He was revealing to Saul that he was already very blind. But his blindness came from within...from within his own heart and mind.

Later on, Paul would tell King Agrippa that he had not been disobedient to the heavenly vision. This was after telling Agrippa the story of the conversion on the road to Damascus. Paul actually calls it a heavenly *vision*. God had to physically blind Saul of Tarsus in order to give him a heavenly vision.

Before this experience, Saul would not listen. He could not see what God was doing with His church because he was obsessed with his own religious zeal. Later on in his letter to the Corinthian church he gives them the name of this particular malady: He called it a veil! "But whenever it turns to the Lord, the veil is taken away" (2 Cor. 3:16).

Now in those days physical veils were in use in the middle east (and are even used today). But in the modern western world, we don't use them much. So I am going to take the liberty to change this word to a more modern and relevant term: a *filter*.

So what is a filter? I'm glad you asked. In this context, a filter is simply a veil or hindrance that lies over your heart or mind that gets in the way of you seeing the Lord clearly. The filter is a mental, emotional, or spiritual blockage that hinders true spiritual sight.

The Problems with a Filter

The first and foremost problem with a filter is that you don't know that you have one—everyone else can see it but you. To them it is obvious in everything you do and say. You just can't see it. But the truth is that if you have been a Christian for any length of time you most likely have several filters. Brothers and sisters, these things must be dealt with by God. But first we must see them for what they are and reject them. Let's take a look at some people who had filters in the scriptures.

Well we have already seen that Paul had many filters he acquired by being a religious zealot. He even lists some of them in this passage:

> I could, of course, put my trust in such things. If any of you think you can trust in external ceremonies, I have even more reason to feel that way. I was circumcised when I was a week old. I am an Israelite by birth, of the tribe of Benjamin, a pure-blooded Hebrew. As far as keeping the Jewish Law is concerned, I was a Pharisee, and I was so zealous that I persecuted the church. As far as a person can be righteous by obeying the commands of the Law, I was without fault. But all those things that I might count as profit I now reckon as loss for Christ's sake. Not only those things; I reckon everything as complete loss for the sake of what is so much more valuable, the knowledge of Christ Jesus my Lord. For his sake I have thrown everything away; I consider it all as mere garbage, so that I may gain Christ and be completely united with him (Phil. 3:4-9).

We can see within this passage that though Paul had many veils (or filters) that caused him to be a religious Jewish zealot, after the Lord Jesus met him on the road to Damascus, everything completely changed. Now, he tells us that he considers everything else as garbage (or *dung* in the original language) compared to knowing and gaining this wonderfully glorious Christ!

What about Peter? Did he have any filters? Oh, yeah.

> From that time on Jesus began to say plainly to his disciples, "I must go to Jerusalem and suffer much from the elders, the chief priests, and the teachers of the Law. I will be put to death, but three days later I will be raised to life." Peter took him aside and began to rebuke him. "God forbid it, Lord!' he said. "That must never happen to you!" Jesus turned around and said to Peter, "Get away from me, Satan! You are an obstacle in my way, because these thoughts of yours don't come from God, but from human nature" (Matt. 16:21-23).

What was going on here? Jesus was revealing that He would be crucified and resurrected three days later. However, all that Peter heard was that Jesus was going to die. This did not fit into Peter's filter at all. You see, Peter (like most Jews in those days) had the filter of the rabbinical teachings that the Messiah would come, overthrow the Roman empire, and then setup God's kingdom on the earth. If Jesus truly was the Messiah then He would be establishing the literal kingdom of God and beginning ruling forever on the earth. The Lord's statement that He was going to die just didn't fit into that plan.

Because of this veil (or filter), Peter needed to be rebuked by the Lord. It's interesting to me the Lord's verbiage here: "these thought of yours don't come from God, but from human nature."

Martha of Bethany also had a filter.

> When Martha heard that Jesus was coming, she went out to meet him, but Mary stayed in the house. Martha said to Jesus, "If you had been here, Lord, my brother would not have died! But I know that even now God will give you whatever you ask him for." "Your brother will rise to life," Jesus told her. "I know," she replied, "that he will rise to life on the last day."

Jesus said to her, "I am the resurrection and the life. Those who believe in me will live, even though they die; and those who live and believe in me will never die. Do you believe this?" "Yes, Lord!" she answered. "I do believe that you are the Messiah, the Son of God, who was to come into the world" (John 11:20-27).

Here we see that Martha is simply quoting to Christ some of the rabbinical teachings going around at the time about an event called "resurrection." It was a belief that all of the Jewish people would one day be brought back from the dead on the earth. Notice with me that Martha did not answer the Lord's question. After telling her that HE was the resurrection and that those who believe in Him would never die, she responds with "Yes, I believe that you are the Messiah." But that wasn't what the Lord asked her. He asked her if she believed that He was the resurrection!

Here again, this kind of filter comes from teachings. But filters can also come from other sources, such as attitudes. Let's take a look at another filter that we see in the disciples.

And it happened in the fulfilling of the days of His taking up, even He set His face to go to Jerusalem. And He sent messengers before His face. And going they went into a village of Samaritans, so as to make ready for Him. And they did not receive Him, because His face was going toward Jerusalem. And seeing His disciples, James and John, said, "Lord, do You desire that we tell fire to come down from Heaven, and to destroy them even as Elijah did?" But turning He rebuked them. And He said, "You do not know of what spirit you are. For the

Son of Man did not come to destroy men's lives, but to save."
And they went to another village (Luke 9:51-56).

Here, we see an attitude that the disciples had concerning those who were not a part of their particular group. An attitude of superiority over others. An attitude of "they are not part of our group, therefore they have no right to exist." In other words, a sectarian attitude. Jesus called this a"spirit" and this seems to imply satanic influence.

But there are many other "filters" that can infiltrate our lives, caused by many things. In Luke chapter fourteen, he covers several more of them.

And one of those reclining with Him, hearing these things, he said to Him, "Blessed are those eating bread in the kingdom of God." But He said to him, "A certain man made a great supper and invited many. And he sent his slave at the supper hour to say to those who had been invited, 'Come, for now all is ready.' And all with one mind began to beg off. The first said to him, 'I have bought a field, and I have need to go out and see it; I ask you, have me excused.' And another said, 'I bought five yoke of oxen and I am going to try them out; I ask you, have me excused.' And another said, 'I married a wife, and for this reason I am not able to come.' And having come up that slave reported these things to his lord. Then being angry, the housemaster said to his slave, 'Go out quickly into the streets and lanes of the city, and bring in here the poor and maimed and lame and blind ones.' And the slave said, 'Sir, it has been done as you ordered, and still there is room.' And the lord said to the slave, 'Go out into the highways and hedges and compel them to come in, so that my house may be filled. For I say to you that not one of those men who had been invited shall taste of my supper.' And great crowds came together to Him." And turning, He said to them, "if anyone comes to Me and does not hate his father, and mother, and wife, and children, and brothers and sisters, and besides, even his own life, he cannot be My disciple. And whoever does not bear his cross and come after Me, he cannot be My disciple" (Luke 14:15-27).

We can see here in this passage that many things can cause "filters" to block our vision of the Lord and His eternal purpose. The aquisition of property, materialism, consumerism, family, and many other things. Our culture is a big one! How much influence does our culture have upon us? Remember that this world system is under the influence of the evil one. "We know that we are from God and that the whole world lies under the control of the evil one" (1 John 5:19).

So, if the whole world system lies under satan, this includes all of the sub-systems of the world such as the governmental system, the political system, the educational system, the business system, the medical system, the religious system, and on and on it goes. All of these influences in our lives can sometimes build subtle filters that blind us to the Lord and His purpose. We, as believers, must be careful that we do not get too caught up into any of these systems. Why? Because we are not a part of the world system! Our kingdom is not of this world! And our King has told us to invest everything we have and everything we are in that kingdom of the heavenlies.

Don't ever worry and say, "What are we going to eat?" or "What are we going to drink?" or "What are we going to wear?" Everyone is concerned about these things, and your heavenly Father certainly knows you need all of them. But first, be concerned about his kingdom and what has His approval. Then all these things will be provided for you (Matt. 6:31-33).

The Heart of the Matter

So let me ask you the baseline question: What are *your* filters, or what has blinded (veiled) you?

Is it some kind of Christian teaching? Are you blinded by the end times, speaking in tongues, spiritual gifts, studying and memorizing the Bible, prayer, evangelism, social action, spiritual warfare, discipleship, authoritarianism, going to church on Sunday, pastoral leadership, or any of the other seemingly endless barrage of Christian teachings and practices?

The difficulty in being able to see your filters is that the filters themselves make you blind to all else. You cannot see clearly if you have a blindfold on. Dropping all of your filters, religious baggage, and agendas is absolutely essential to beginning to learn how to "see" Christ as your all in all. Please understand that to the degree that you let go of those filters, that will be the degree that you press in to know your Lord deeply. It's like the burial wrappings that Lazarus had around him. Even though he was raised from the dead by the Lord Jesus, he still needed to discard those "wrappings" to be totally free to live for Him. Those "wrappings" were actually "trappings" that would hinder him from walking freely if he did not remove them. It is interesting that Lazarus himself did not remove the burial wrappings—others did it. Many times the Lord will use other brothers and sisters from within His Body to reveal these things to you. But are you humble enough to receive from them?

No, the whole matter is summed up into seeing Jesus; and when you really see Jesus, what happens? What happened to Saul of Tarsus? Well, a whole lot of things happened, and mighty things which nothing else would have accomplished. You would never have argued Saul of Tarsus into Christianity; you would never have frightened him into Christianity; you would never have either reasoned or emotionalized him into being a Christian. To get that man out of Judaism needed something more than could have been found on this earth. But he saw Jesus of Nazareth, and that did it. He is out, he is an emancipated man, he has seen.

T. Austin-Sparks, *Spiritual Sight*

Free From Filters

Now, how do we become free of filters, religious baggage and agendas? There is only one way that I know of.

You must humble yourself in the sight of the Lord.

Trust me, the Lord knows all about all of your baggage. First you must be willing to admit that you have baggage (we all do, by the way). Then ask Him to reveal these things to you. Of course, this must be done in totally honesty between you and your Lord. But after you do this, hang on for a somewhat scary ride because if you maintain your honesty and openness with the Lord, He will begin to show you things you never even imagined. The key here is not to get defensive and just let the love of God pour over you as He reveals these things to you. He will do this in a completely loving, caring, and gentle way, but it will still hurt! That is, it will hurt in an emotional and mental way. It will hurt your pride, mostly. But that's okay. That is something that needs to be "hurt" anyway. None of us have it together as much as we think we do. You may have been a Christian for fifty years and yet not really know Him very well at all. You may have been a leader of some sort and been in Christian ministry for decades but don't really know

Him. Please understand that its only to the degree that you let the Lord deal with you concerning the veils that you will come to know Him in a deep and intimate way.

The Most Deceptive Filter

At the foundation of all filters is a root cause. You could say that this is the reason (or culprit) for the way that filters attach themselves over your spiritual eyes and block your clear vision of our Lord. And that reason is *your self*! "For whoever may desire to save his life will lose it. But whoever may lose his life for My sake will find it" (Matt. 16:25).

This "self-life" must be dealt with by the Lord or your filters will remain in tact and your spiritual vision and perception will be crippled, to say the least. The first step is for you to honestly and humbly come before your Lord and ask Him to reveal these things to you. And then...be willing to receive what He tells you. Believe me, this will definitely hurt. The self has been deceived into believing that the filters are part of your person. But this is a lie of the evil one. Those filters have attached themselves to you like parasites that have been feeding off of your pride, arrogance, greed, insecurity, and lack of trust in the Lord. They are not a part of you! They are not your identity! You have a new identity in Christ and those filters are not a part of it!

If you will turn to the Lord Jesus in humility and simplicity (like a child) He will begin to deal with your filters, religious baggage, and agendas. "But whenever someone turns to the Lord, the veil is taken away" (2 Cor. 3:16).

Chapter Eight

Seeing the Unseen

That's why we are not discouraged. No, even if outwardly we are wearing out, inwardly we are being renewed each and every day. This light, temporary nature of our suffering is producing for us an everlasting weight of glory, far beyond any comparison, because we do not look for things that can be seen but for things that cannot be seen. For things that can be seen are temporary, but things that cannot be seen are eternal (2 Cor. 4:16-18).

Here we can see several important principals that will help us to understand true spiritual sight. First of all, Paul and his co-workers were not discouraged. How can this be? Do you realize what this man went through? Let me list a few of the trials that he refers to.

...but in everything commending ourselves as servants of God, in much endurance, in afflictions, in hardships, in distresses, in beatings, in imprisonments, in tumults, in labors, in sleeplessness, in hunger, in purity, in knowledge, in patience, in kindness, in the Holy Spirit, in genuine love, in the word of truth, in the power of God; by the weapons of righteousness for the right hand and the left, by glory and dishonor, by evil report and good report; regarded as deceivers and yet true; as unknown yet well-known, as dying yet behold, we live; as punished yet not put to death, as sorrowful yet always rejoicing, as poor yet making many rich, as having nothing yet possessing all things (2 Cor. 6:5-10).

Are they servants of Christ?—I speak as if insane—I more so; in far more labors, in far more imprisonments, beaten times without number, often in danger of death. Five times I received from the Jews thirty-nine lashes. Three times I was beaten with rods, once I was stoned, three times I was shipwrecked, a night and a day I have spent in the deep. I have been on frequent journeys, in dangers from rivers, dangers from robbers, dangers from my countrymen, dangers from the Gentiles, dangers in the city, dangers in the wilderness, dangers on the sea, dangers among false brethren; I have been in labor and hardship, through many sleepless nights, in hunger and thirst, often without food, in cold and exposure. Apart from such external things, there is the daily pressure on me of concern for all the churches (2 Cor. 11:23-28).

But yet after all of this Paul tells us that he and his co-workers were not discouraged! This is because they were not looking at the things which are seen, but those that are unseen. Brothers and sisters, the things which are unseen are what's important! They are the eternal things. We must all learn to see with our inward eyes and not just the eyes of flesh. If not, we will get bogged down in discouragement and disappointment. Let's face it, the things we see (physically) around us don't look too promising. Yet Christ is building His unseen kingdom inside of each one of us. But what are we looking at? The world system? The religious system? Unfaithful Christians all around us?

Paul was a brother who truly learned to see the unseen (remember, he had a heavenly vision that governed his whole life). Here was a man who was totally entrenched in the Judaic system of the temple, the priesthood, the rituals, and yet he was able to see it for what it truly was: a temporary foreshadow of that which was to come, the true eternal New Jerusalem. And this is what he shares with us in the letter to the Hebrews.

> For you have not come to a mountain that can be touched and to a blazing fire, and to darkness and gloom and whirlwind, and to the blast of a trumpet and the sound of words which sound was such that those who heard begged that no further word be spoken to them (Heb. 12:18, 19).

> But you have come to Mount Zion and to the city of the living God, the heavenly Jerusalem, and to myriads of angels, to the general assembly and church of the firstborn who are enrolled in heaven, and to God, the Judge of all, and to the spirits of the

righteous made perfect, and to Jesus, the mediator of a new
covenant, and to the sprinkled blood, which speaks better than
the blood of Abel (Heb. 12:22-24).

The Issue of Our Focus

When we are dealing with seeing and experiencing the Lord in a deeper way, we must cover the subject of focus. Here are several definitions
for the word as a noun and as a verb:

Focus (n): *a central point, as of attraction, attention, or activity; the
clear and sharply defined condition of an image*

Focus (v): *to direct one's attention or efforts; to be or become focused*

In life, we become like the things we focus on. For example, people who focus on negative things will become negative people. People
who focus on the positive will become people who are uplifting and a
pleasure to be with. People who are fixated on automobiles will always
be thinking and talking about automobiles. That which is your focus
will not only consume you but will also change you.

But what determines your focus? Is it not that which you *value*
the most? You will always focus on those things which are the most
important to you. Those things which you value the most will be at
the top of your list, so to speak. Those things which you value less will
be further down the list. So, the big question is: *What do you value
the most?*

But store up for yourselves treasures in heaven, where neither
moth nor rust destroys, and where thieves do not break in or
steal; **for where your treasure is, there your heart will be also.**

The eye is the lamp of the body; so then if your eye is clear, your whole body will be full of light. But if your eye is bad, your whole body will be full of darkness. If then the light that is in you is darkness, how great is the darkness! No one can serve two masters; for either he will hate the one and love the other, or he will be devoted to one and despise the other. You cannot serve God and wealth (Matt. 6:20-24).

And right here, my brothers and sisters, is the main problem with many Christians. They themselves (the self) still hold the central place in their own lives! They have never truly allowed Jesus Christ to be the center, the head, and the life of them. In other words, they have not yet made Him Lord of all. If this issue is not settled in the life of the believer, then Christ will only ever have a nominal place in their focus. And that is why we see so little change among God's people. Oh, they might believe the correct doctrines and go to church and contribute to the offering plate. But their lives really have not gone through any significant (or even radical) change. And believe me, being a Christian is an extremely radical thing! This lack of change (or transformation) is because of a lack of focus on the Lord Jesus Christ. Oh, yes, we love to focus on Christ "things." We love to focus on ministry, Christian music, Christian television, etc. But I am talking about the giving of our undivided attention to a person! I have to say, unfortunately, that after having been a Christian for over four decades and knowing many believers, there is definitely a gross lack of focus on the person of Jesus Christ Himself.

"He is also head of the body, the church; and He is the beginning, the firstborn from the dead, so that **He Himself** will come to have first place in everything" (Col 1:18). First place in *everything*! Dear believer, does Jesus Christ have the first place in everything in your life? Does He have the central place of focus in your life? If not, then it will be very difficult (if not impossible) for you to learn the lessons contained in the remainder of this book. How will you be able to learn how to intensely gaze upon Him (or "behold" Him) if He is not the main focus of your whole life?

The quote I gave you at the beginning of this chapter was from 2 Cor. 4:16-18. In this passage, Paul tells us that he and his co-workers did not even look for the things which are seen but only those things which are unseen. Now, you might be thinking, *well, Milt, this sounds kind of spooky.* Actually, it's not at all spooky or hyper-spiritual. It's absolutely normal! Looking constantly at all the seen (visible) things around us is an abnormal lifestyle. You see, Paul and his associates were simply living the normal Christian life. In our minds we think that these guys were super spiritual giants, but really they were just normal believers living by the life of Christ. Modern day Christianity has become so sub-normal that now we think that just living the normal Christian life is being a spiritual giant.

So, dear brother and dear sister, where are you at in all of this? Hopefully at this point you are asking the question, *how do I make Christ my only passion and focus?* Well, thankfully, it's really very simple. Get into a solitary place and do some business with your Lord. Stop reading this book right now and get into a quiet place and finally give up all rights to your own life. Talk to your Lord. Make Him your all in all. Completely lay down your life once and for all to Him. Hold back nothing. Surrender completely. Be completely open and honest with Him. He loves you with an unending love.

Chapter Nine

Seeing Christ in All Things

Now we are going to get more practical concerning seeing our Lord Jesus with our spiritual eyes (our spirits). In previous chapters, I set some groundwork for the importance of spiritual sight and beholding Christ in our spirits, and also gave a very brief revelation of Christ and the importance of knowing Him as He is instead of how we see Him through our own lenses. Now, I would like to begin to cover some of the ways that we can see Him in our daily lives, and introduce the value of the individual believer.

This chapter is simply an introduction to seeing Christ in all things. The chapters following will go into more detail and give many practical helps.

Please understand here that my heart in presenting some of these things is not to give you "methods" per se. However, I do want to get practical. Balancing these two is not an easy task. I will be sharing some of the things that I do in order to help you put these things into practice. They are for the purpose of example only and not to try and institute some kind of hard-and-fast rules. By providing examples from my own life (and the lives of others), it will help you to understand how to practically apply these things to your own life. They may not happen the same way for you and, of course, that is perfectly fine.

The Importance of the Individual Believer

It only makes sense that the body (expression) of Christ will only be as strong as each individual member of that body. That's why God placed His Son into every one of us—so that each one of us would have the inward strength and ability to display His Son. You, as a member of His Body, can now draw from His life and character so that you can display this life. It is important to know that this is both an *individual* walk and a *corporate* walk.

While both aspects have value and importance, most of Christianity down through the centuries has emphasized only the personal (individual) walk and not the corporate. But if you read the scriptures carefully (with insight from the Spirit), you will see that God wants the corporate thing, too.

"The man Jesus has now been made both Lord and Christ" (Acts 2:36). This verse is very interesting indeed. What does it mean "both Lord and Christ?" The word "Lord" comes from the Greek word *kurios* which means having power or authority. It can also be translated as "master" or "owner." Simply stated in today's terms, it means the *one in charge*. Jesus Christ is now the Lord of all, He is the one in charge. The word "Christ" means the anointed One (anointed with the Holy Spirit). And it is this Christ, the Holy-Spirit-anointed one in charge, who now resides inside of believers. But why?

It's because of the *hope of glory* (see Col. 1:24-29). But what is glory? This word is difficult to describe but I will do my best according to the understanding the Lord has given me.

In a nutshell, it means *expression* or *manifestation*. You see, our God wants to express all that He is and has. He wants to display His character, His nature, His power, and His attributes. But since our God is a corporate God (Father, Son, and Spirit), He can only fully express Himself through a corporate vessel. Hence, we see Paul's revelation of "Christ in you the hope of glory." It's important to understand that in this verse the word "you" is plural (remember that Paul is writing here to a corporate people, the church in Colossae). It's literally: "Christ in *you all*, the hope of glory."

A corporate God wants to have a corporate expression. That only makes sense. However, the process of the members of His body becoming that corporate expression is actually a very complex one. In order for His expression to be a true and pure one it must come from transformed vessels. As we all know, the church of Jesus Christ is made up of many very imperfect people!

Even though we all have Christ living inside of us, our old man (the flesh) is also living inside of us. There is a battle of sorts going on inside of you between the old man (the flesh) and the new man (Christ in you). The problem is that our God wants an image of Himself in corporate form. But the only way that God can get this in reality and power is through something called *transformation* happening in each individual. This word can also be translated as being transfigured. In Matthew's gospel he tells us that Jesus took Peter, James, and John with Him up to the mount and was *transfigured* before them. Kenneth Wuest has an excellent literal translation of the event.

> And after six days, Jesus takes with Him Peter, and James, and John, and brings them up into a mountain, a high one, in private, alone. And the manner of His outward expression was changed before them, that outward expression coming from and being truly representative of His inner nature. And His garments became glittering ones, exceedingly white, such as a fuller on earth is not able thus to whiten (Matt. 17:1-2).

You can also think of glory in this way. A fruit tree goes through different seasons. All four seasons of spring, summer, fall, and winter bring different changes to the tree. In the wintertime, it doesn't appear that there is much happening with the tree, at least not outwardly. But inside of the tree it's a different story. There is life flowing and strengthening the tree for the coming growing season. And later there is the season of fruit-bearing when we can all benefit from the results. But the season when the tree is the most beautiful is during the springtime when it's in full bloom. The flowers are an awesome display (or expression) of the life within the tree. We could say the blossoms are the "glory" of the tree.

In both examples, we can see that the outward expression (or glory) came from, and was truly representative of, the inner nature. That's what God is after! He wants a people who are so changed, transfigured, and transformed into His image that their outward expression is truly representative of their inner nature. And what is that inner nature? Christ, Christ, and only Christ!

Time with the Lord Daily

I see our spiritual lives with the Lord in two ways: the daily and the moment by moment.

I (and many others) have found the best way to know the Lord in an ongoing way is to have special, undistracted time with Him each day. Let's call this our "daily time with the Lord." Of course I realize that all of our time is actually with the Lord, but what I am calling here the "daily time with the Lord" is a designated time each day when you spend undistracted time with your glorious Christ.

In the scriptures (and throughout history), we can see the saints of old spending time with God apart from others. The saints in the Old Testament did this. In the New Testament, Jesus Christ is a perfect example of one who would get away to spend time with His Father. For Jesus, this usually took place in the first part of the day—in the morning. Personally, I also like the morning as a time to spend alone with God. There are several reasons why I believe this is the best time. It's the *first* of the day so it's the easiest time to give the Lord your total focus because you are normally the most refreshed in the morning. (Now, please understand that when I say "morning" I am referring to the first part of your day. The actual time of day may vary according to your own schedule. But the point is that this will be the first part of *your* day no matter what time it is according to the clock.)

Of course, you can do this at any time throughout the day. The point is that this time is set aside and is a very focused time for you to be with Him. But it is not, and must not be, the only time!

Please do not approach this "daily time with the Lord" as some kind of religious duty. It's not that at all. It's not an obligation—it's a privilege. You get to spend wonderful time with your wonderful Lord!

Also, please understand that you do not have to do this. It's not a law. However, in my own (and in many other believers') experience I can tell you that if you back off or ignore this time altogether, your spiritual life will definitely suffer. You will still be in Christ, and He will still be in you. He will still love you, and you will still be all that you are in Him. But the spiritual outworking of the expression of Christ through you will suffer for it. Please let me explain that statement.

If you are a believer, then you have Jesus the Christ living inside of you. This is a spiritual reality. The reason that God placed His Son inside of you is for two reasons: 1.) so that His eternal purpose would be fulfilled, and 2.) so that you will have the power, character, and strength to live by His life.

As stated already in this book, God's eternal purpose is that He would have a vessel, a vehicle, an expression to display the fullness of His Son. This vessel would be a corporate expression of His Son. Just as the Trinity expresses God corporately, so the church would express the Son corporately. This is so that the whole world and the whole creation (visible and invisible) would see and experience this totally wonderful Christ.

My dear brothers and sisters, for this to happen there must be time spent in the holy of holies before the Lord. This is essential to everything else. Do you actually think that you could spend time in the presence of the living God and not be changed? And the more you are changed on the inside the more you will be transformed on the outside. And when many people are changed in this way, then God will have His purpose of a body, a bride, a house, a city, a kingdom, a new man (humanity), and a new creation expressing His nature, His life, and His power in all of creation!

Time with the Lord Moment by Moment

Now we are discussing our moment-by-moment relationship and fellowship with the Lord who lives inside of us. In fact, this is why He lives inside of us—so we can be with Him at all times and in all places. Talk about mobility! Talk about convenience! You are infinitely more connected to Him than even your cell phone. You can lose that. You can run out of battery. But He is continuously in you and with you. What a Christ! And how convenient is that? He told us that He would always be with us and would never leave us. Now the question is: are we taking advantage of that wonderful fact? Are we turning to Him moment by moment or only during our "prayer time" or when we are "in church?" You see, this is what separates the men from the boys (so to speak). Are we *abiding* or are we running in and out of His presence? Are we remaining in the awareness and practice of His presence or are we just coming to visit when we have the time?

My goal here is not to place you under any kind of religious guilt, pressure, or condemnation. But I do wish to stir up something that is deep within your spirit. I am assuming that you are reading this book because you love God and want to know Him in a deep and abiding way. I am appealing to that part of you. He wants a much deeper relationship with you than you ever imagined. Therefore, there is great hope in the fact that your God wants this much more than you do. There is no lack of desire on His part.

God wants us to fellowship with Him every moment of every day!

Dwell in Me, and I will dwell in you. [Live in Me, and I will live in you.] Just as no branch can bear fruit of itself without abiding in (being vitally united to) the vine, neither can you bear fruit unless you abide in Me. I am the Vine; you are the branches. Whoever lives in Me and I in him bears much (abundant) fruit. However, apart from Me [cut off from vital union with Me] you can do nothing (John 15:4-5).

Here, the word "abide" means to *remain* or *live in*. God has not called us to merely spend time with Him. He has called us to live in Him! We all know that He lives in us and we *live in Him*, but that can just be a location. For example, my location right now is Eckert, Colorado. It's where I live. But abiding means much more than merely *living in*. Even though I live in Colorado, it doesn't mean that I am abiding in Colorado. Abiding is a much deeper word. It means to take full advantage of, enjoy, relish in, immerse myself in, enjoy the fullness thereof, take in and experience all that Colorado has to offer.

Dear saint, are you living in Christ like that? Or are you going about the daily business of life, saying your prayers, and going to church? Isn't life more than that? Isn't God's eternal purpose for your life more than that? If we cannot get beyond our "quiet time" with the Lord each day and saying our prayers, then we are definitely *not* abiding in Him. It is possible to be in Christ positionally (as all Spirit-born Christians are) and yet not be living or experiencing Christ on a moment-by-moment basis. This is where the growth happens. This is where the transformation takes place. It's by beholding Him that we are transformed (transfigured) into His image from glory to glory. "But we all, with unveiled face, beholding as in a mirror the glory of the Lord, are being transformed into the same image from glory to glory, just as from the Lord, the Spirit" (2 Cor. 3:18).

As I said previously, this word "beholding" is a very deep word. It means much more than simply looking at or seeing. It is a *participation in* and a *fellowship in* a particular object or, in this case, a Person. "Beholding" is not a word we usually use in Christianity. In fact, it may even seem strange to you. But it is an extremely intense and beautiful word and I want to make sure that you have a clear understanding of the word (and more so, of the activity it is) before we proceed much further. (Of course, you will need to ask the Lord Himself to give you clarity and understanding about the wonders of this practice.) Beholding is a deep seeing, a spiritual seeing, and yet it can be very practical as well. I will share more about this throughout the rest of this book.

Chapter Ten

Learning to Behold

Brother Lawrence was a Carmelite monk in Paris, France during the 1600s. He wrote an awesome book called "Practicing His Presence" (and I definitely recommend it). In this book he describes his experience of learning to practice the presence of the Lord, or we could say learning to "behold" Him. Lawrence's responsibility inside of the monastery was called "kp" or the kitchen patrol cleanup. In other words, he washed the dishes. He took it upon himself to use this "kp" time as an opportunity to learn to fellowship with his Lord. Of course, there is much more to the story but that gives you the idea. My question is, are you and I taking advantage of the opportunities that we all have to spend time with the Lord throughout our day? We probably have at least a thousand little moments throughout our day when we can turn and behold Him. Lawrence called this "practicing His presence."

Beholding the Lord Daily

Let's begin by focusing our attention on the first part of the day during our time with the Lord in the morning. I recommend that you start this time by first calming your mind, will, and emotions. Quieting these integrated parts of your soul life will be your biggest challenge. Start, by an act of your will, learning to calm your mind. As we all know, the mind is like a restless wanderer. It wanders all over the place most of the time. So, you will need to get to a quiet and lonely place with the least number of distractions as possible. We see our Lord doing this while He was on the earth. "In the early morning, while it was still dark, Jesus got up, left the house, and went away to a secluded place, and was praying there" Mark 1:35.

I also recommend that you close your eyes (to diminish the distractions) and just sit and be quiet for a while. But this is not a passive time. You will be calming your soul and turning your mind, will, and emotions to your Lord who lives within you. Every time your mind wanders to other things (such as what you will do today, etc.), just bring it back to Christ. Be aware of the glorious fact that Jesus Christ is vibrantly living inside of you right now!

The Power of Silence

"Withdraw yourself for times of listening to silence. Withdraw yourself for times of sweet solitude. And come to avoid the sound of men constantly speaking. And the word of heavenly wisdom will come to you." -*Silence* by John Michael Talbot

Silence is one of your greatest gifts and privileges. It is not only something we desperately need, but also something that will set the stage for our time of beholding. We behold Him in the silence. The problem is that in our day silence is hard to find. We live in a noisy place and time. Now, especially with the prominence of technology, silence is at a premium. We have to struggle to get some peace and quiet; we fight to hear the silence. And yet our Lord is beckoning us to come to the quiet and be with Him. How can He speak to us if we are always listening to noise or making noise ourselves?

So, I recommend starting your time calming your soul. This may take a good amount of time, depending upon how often you have done this. But don't rush it. Believe me, it will be very frustrating at first when you realize how undisciplined your mind, will, and emotions really are. You will find that you need to bring your mind back to Christ over and over and over again. The mind is a wanderer, and it will wander all over the place. This is why Paul tells us the following:

> Therefore if you have been raised up with Christ, keep seeking the things above, where Christ is, seated at the right hand of God. Set your mind on the things above, not on the things that are on earth. For you have died and your life is hidden with Christ in God. When Christ, who is our life, is revealed, then you also will be revealed with Him in glory (Col. 3:1-4).

Notice how he tells us to *set our minds* on things above. With your will you can choose to deliberately set your mind on this or that. This is an act of your will. Don't wait for God to do it. He is waiting for you to do it! Whenever you realize that your mind has wandered again, simply and gently bring it back to the Christ who lives within you. See Him there. Behold Him there. Intensely gaze upon His face. Focus all of your attention on Him and all that He is. When you sense that your mind has wandered again, simply pull it back to Christ. You may need to do this a thousand times during just one session of beholding Him.

But be of good cheer…it will get easier! Practice makes perfect, as they say. Don't get discouraged. The key is to continue on a daily basis and not to give up.

The Power of Focus

Turn your eyes upon Jesus
Look full in his wonderful face
And the things of earth will grow strangely dim
In the light of his glory and grace

As I mentioned in chapter six, this hymn was written by Helen Howarth Lemmel and was inspired by a tract called "Focused" by a missionary named Isabella Lilias Trotter. Here is a quote from that tract:

What does this focusing mean? Study the matter and you will see that it means two things—gathering in all that can be gathered, and letting the rest drop. The working of any lens—microscope, telescope, camera—will show you this. The lens of your own eye, in the room where you are sitting, as clearly as any other. Look at the window bars, and the beyond is only a shadow; look through at the distance, and it is the bars that turn into ghosts. You have to choose which you will fix your gaze upon and let the other go.

When you behold the Lord, you are focusing all of your mind, will, and emotions upon Him. All other matters must fade into the foggy distance. We can really only adequately focus on one thing at a time. When the song says *turn your eyes upon Jesus* it is telling us to turn all of our attention to the Lord who lives inside of us. Again, this is an act of our will. You deliberate to focus all of the attention of your soul to the Lord who lives within your spirit. You really don't need to understand all of this technically. Just focus all of your attention (with your mind, will, and emotions) on the object. Of course, in our case, we are not focusing all of our being upon an object but upon a person. And when we do that, something mysterious and yet very wonderful happens: We are being transformed into the same image as the person we are beholding! Wow! What a Lord! We are changed every time we just look at Him!

The Power of Perseverance

I would like to encourage you because this practice of spending time in the morning with your Lord will take lots of perseverance. This means discipline. Now, you may be thinking, "Well, Milt, that leaves me out. I'm just not a very disciplined person." Well, you're not the only one! None of us is disciplined by nature, and it's only in Christ and by the Holy Spirit that we can become disciplined people. All that He requires of you is that you take the initial step of faith. Get up, get away, and sit there waiting upon the Lord. Tell Him something like this: "Well, Lord, here I am to spend time with only you." Then close your eyes and "see" Him with your spirit. Then love Him. Just love Him.

Speak words of love to Him, such as:

"Lord, I love you so much."
"I am here for only you."
"I give my whole being and life to you, my precious Jesus."
"Give me the strength to focus on only you during this time."
"Lord, you are so beautiful!"

"There is no one like you."

"Your glory and majesty are simply astounding!"

Please note: This time with the Lord will not be primarily for conventional-type prayer. You will not be asking Him for anything. You will not be "pulling on His robe" to get Him to help you in any way other than to have fellowship with you. How would you feel if the only time your children wanted to be with you was to ask you for things? Wouldn't you feel like a "Santa Claus" parent? What kind of a relationship is that? So, you are not there to ask Him for anything. You are there to simply be with Him, behold Him, and love Him! No agendas—just you loving your Lord.

Now during this time of beholding you may sense in your spirit that the Lord wants you to pray for someone or something. Be flexible and free enough to do that. He may even tell you to get up and call someone that you have had an issue with in the past. He may also lead you to the scriptures to continue beholding Him in a certain passage. There are an untold number of things that God may speak to you during your time of beholding Him. Keep your focus on Him but be flexible enough to hear Him in the midst of your fellowship together. There are many things that can come out of your special time of beholding Him.

Actually, you are focusing not only your soul (mind, will, emotions), but also your spirit upon Him. You do this with your will. The will is like the rudder of the ship that you turn this way and that to steer it towards a particular direction. "Turn your eyes upon Jesus" actually means to turn your *whole being* to Him.

Brothers and sisters, this will require lots of practice and an amount of discipline. But the key here is not to give up. Even when you don't sense his presence at all, keep pursuing Him. Some of these beholding times may not produce any tangible fruit at all. But believe me, they are not wasted! All time that you spend in His presence has much more value than you can imagine. We are talking about eternal things here. Spiritual things. Even though you may feel as if nothing is happening, there is great worth and many precious jewels that are being formed inside of you.

Beholding the Lord in the Scriptures

This is one of the most precious and yet also most abused ways to "see" your Lord. The problem is that most of us modern-day Christians have been through one or more religious movements. It is not within the scope of this book to discuss those movements in great detail. However, I will need to refer to at least one of them in order to explain some of the problems associated with them. But before I do, let me say that all of these movements were inspired by the Holy Spirit to some degree. The problem is that men got their hands on them and then they became polluted. As a result, the movement had a toxic element to it that could be spiritually harmful. Unfortunately, when God moves, men put their hands on it for their own self interests—to build their own little kingdoms, so to speak.

There was a movement that came eventually to be called "fundementalism." The intention behind the leaders of this movement was to protect Christians from the errors of false doctrine. The problem was that, like most things, the pendulum swung the other way and that desire to "guard the Word" became an unholy thing that made the Bible the center of everything, forgetting that the whole purpose of the scriptures is to bring us to the person of Jesus Christ. "You search the Scriptures because you think that in them you have eternal life; it is these that testify about Me; and you are unwilling to come to Me so that you may have life" (John 5:39-40).

The purpose of the scriptures is to bring us to Christ, in whom we have eternal life. We do not have life in the scriptures themselves. Eternal life can only be found in this wonderfully glorious person that we read about in the scriptures. We need to learn how to use the scriptures in a meditative and inward way. If we combine beholding or "meditation" with reading the scriptures, we will discover a whole new way to experience the Lord. "Experiencing the Depths of Jesus Christ" by Jeanne Guyon can be a great help in this matter. Here, she compares beholding Christ in the scriptures to eating food in the natural:

> When, then, we are thus buried in ourselves, and deeply penetrated with the presence of God within us—when the senses are all drawn from the circumference to the center, which, though it is not easily accomplished at first, becomes quite natural afterwards—when the soul is thus gathered up within itself, and is sweetly occupied with the truth read, not in reasoning upon it, but in feeding upon it, and exciting the will by the affection rather than the understanding by consideration: the affection being thus touched, must be suffered to repose sweetly and at peace, swallowing what it has tasted.
>
> As a person who only masticated an excellent meat would not be nourished by it, although he would be sensible of its taste, unless he ceased this movement in order to swallow it; so when the affection is stirred, if we seek continually to stir it, we extinguish its fire, and thus deprive the soul of its nourishment. We must swallow by a loving repose (full of respect and confidence) what we have masticated and tasted. This method is

very necessary, and would advance the soul in a short time
more than any other would do in several years.

"O taste and see that the LORD is good; How blessed is the man who takes refuge in Him" (Psalms 34:8).

There is a time for study of the scriptures, but this is not that time. This is a time of devotion, affection, and lovingly consuming the words of our Lord. Here, we are not seeking to be educated nor to understand with our minds, but rather, to breath-in and enjoy Him. Another way of stating this is *praying the scriptures or turning scripture into prayer and worship.*

Let's take a small portion of scripture as an example.

Therefore if you have been raised up with Christ, keep seeking the things above, where Christ is, seated at the right hand of God. Set your mind on the things above, not on the things that are on earth. For you have died and your life is hidden with Christ in God. When Christ, who is our life, is revealed, then you also will be revealed with Him in glory (Col. 3:1-4).

One example of a possible prayer or worship declaration to go with this scripture:

"Lord Jesus, thank you so much that I have been raised up with you in resurrection life! You are my all, my life, and my resurrection. Right now, I am seated with you in the heavenly places! Hallelujah! I set my mind upon you, not on the things of this earth or the world system. For because of your death and my inclusion into that death I am free of such things. And now my only life is being inside of you. Thank you, Lord, that you will reveal your glory and that all of your chosen ones are part of that glory!"

You may be thinking right now, "Hey, Milt, I can't do that. I'm not an author like you." But that is not true. You have the living Christ inside of you and all you have to do is let your spirit do the talking. Just start out with something simple and short. It doesn't have to be anything as elaborate as my example above. This takes practice and the more you do it the easier it will become. Trust me.

Partnering

Why not take the above exercise and try it with another believer? One of you can read the passage slowly and clearly. Then spend a little time silently before the Lord with a few words of love and praise. Then, as your spirit leads, begin to pray these scriptures. You will find that this flows very beautifully after a short time of practice. While one of you speaks to the Lord, the other will be inspired to speak things based on what was shared previously. This bouncing off of one another is how the body functions, whether it is just two saints or many.

Beholding the Lord Moment by Moment

Now that we have taken a look at beholding the Lord in our special time with Him and in the scriptures, let's take a look at beholding Him throughout the whole day.

Unfortunately, most of us Christians have a "convience store" kind of God. That is, we run to Him at certain times throughout our week, mostly when we need something from Him. But that is not the kind of relationship that our Lord wants to have with us. He is looking for a people who will be with Him more and more throughout every minute of every day.

Abide in Me, and I in you. As the branch cannot bear fruit of itself unless it abides in the vine, so neither can you unless you abide in Me. I am the vine, you are the branches; he who abides in Me and I in him, he bears much fruit, for apart from Me you can do nothing. If anyone does not abide in Me, he is thrown away as a branch and dries up; and they gather them, and cast them into the fire and they are burned. If you abide in Me, and My words abide in you, ask whatever you wish, and it will be done for you. My Father is glorified by this, that you bear much fruit, and so prove to be My disciples (John 15:4-8).

As I shared in the previous chapter, the word "abide" literally means to *remain*. Our Lord is telling us here that He wants us to remain in constant fellowship with Him. He doesn't want a people who are running in and out of Him when they need something. He wants a people who are always with Him, remaining (staying) with Him on a constant basis. This word also means to "continue in," "to remain inside," and "to continue with."

I think that you will agree that our Lord wants more than just your prayer time! You see, the only way that you can bear fruit is by abiding. Who ever heard of a branch that was fruitful by jumping on and off of the vine all the time? No, our God is in the business of building a kingdom where His Son is the center, life, power, and head of His body. To put it another way, He is growing a vineyard. He is the vine and we are the branches. He cannot get His kingdom/body without that abiding. So, it is absolutely essential that we all learn how to behold this glorious Christ all throughout the day.

Mission: Impossible

But how is it possible to behold the Lord all day? We all have to live on this planet. We all have to work, raise families, drive cars, and on and on it goes. How can we fellowship with God through all of this thing that we call daily life? How can we abide with and in Christ in the middle of all these distractions that the world has to offer? We can't all be monks like Brother Lawrence! Ah, very true indeed. But what if I told you that there is a way to learn how to behold this Lord on a moment-by-moment basis even in the midst of the busiest of lives? Actually, it's a very simple thing called turning.

Turning is taking one small moment and *remembering Him* when you are performing any task (no matter how much of your attention it may take). It is simply the act of refocusing your mind, will, and emotions to the living Christ who dwells within you.

> But to this day whenever Moses is read, a veil lies over their heart; **but whenever a person turns to the Lord**, the veil is taken away. Now the Lord is the Spirit, and where the Spirit of the Lord is, there is liberty. But we all, with unveiled face, beholding as in a mirror the glory of the Lord, are being transformed into the same image from glory to glory, just as from the Lord, the Spirit (2 Cor. 3:15-18).

Notice that it's whenever a person turns to the Lord that the veil of self, sin, religion, and the world system is taken away. This is extremely important! Here again, it's all about focus. The problem is that most of the time we are focused on ourselves. This is the dilemma of the soul-life. Because we are fallen creatures, the soul-life still has more sway over us than the spirit life. So our natural tendencies are to behold the flesh instead of Christ inside of our spirits. But I have some good news! God in Christ has now changed all of that forever. He has given us a spirit and now those who are His have the living Christ inside of them. And because of this glorious fact we now have a choice. We can still live on in the flesh if we choose to. But we can also live on in the spirit if we choose to. It's all a matter of turning. And that is a matter of the will. The human will is like the rudder on a ship. The will can choose to go any direction it desires. This is the power of free will that our Lord has given every human. You can think of it as a football team. If you choose to go the way of the flesh then the team of human lusts, sin, and selfishness will back you. But if you choose to go the way of the spirit, then the Father, Son, and Spirit will back you. Which team do you want backing you?

The Science of Turning

You will need to turn to the Lord hundreds (maybe thousands) of times per day. By now you should have discovered that when you sit down and attempt to behold nothing else but the Lord how quickly your mind begins to wander to other things. This is even more true throughout your day. Of course, it only makes sense. You are bound to be more distracted when you are out and about your day than when you are sitting down and having your focused time with Him in the beginning of your day. But yet the Lord is with you in this whole "turning" business! Just ask Him to remind you when you are distracted away from Him. Of course, we all have things we have to do every day and some of those things take lots of our attention. But here is a secret. It is possible to function in your daily tasks with your mind and yet be focusing on Christ with your spirit. How? I'm glad you asked.

This is where the practice of *turning* comes into play. Take a moment to:

Remember who your Lord is.

Remember that He is so glorious.

Remember that He is so wonderful.

Remember that He is God of heaven and earth.

Remember that He loves you.

Remember just one thing He has done.

Remember His humility.

Remember His loving-kindness.

Remember His glorious victory over death.

Remember that this Christ lives in you right now.

Or, it might just be a quick moment when you just say His name.

You can turn by simply remembering Him in these very simple ways. This can be done all throughout your day. Do you realize how much down time you have every day? All of us have times throughout our day when we are doing something that doesn't really require much (or any) of our attention. How about sitting in an airport? Walking through the grocery store? Taking a shower? Driving to work? Taking a walk? Waiting for a bus? Waiting for anything? Why not use these times to turn to Him who lives within your spirit? Take advantage of these little "commas" in your time by turning to the Lord and fellowshipping with Him.

I love that Paul states very clearly in 2 Corinthians 3:18 that when we turn to the Lord and behold Him, we are changed (transfigured) into His image from glory to glory. Every time we behold Him, we are transformed a little bit more. Wow! What a Christ! That's how glorious He is. That's how powerful He is. So dear saint, please never think that any time spent turning to Him is ever wasted. Do not take these moments lightly. They are incredibly valuable in your progress of learning to behold. It takes practice. But the more you practice, the more you are being transformed.

I also really like how Paul describes the turning process. First there is the turning, then there is the beholding: "...but whenever a person turns to the Lord, the veil is taken away" (2 Cor. 3:15).

Remember that unless the veil is taken away you cannot see your Lord. This is the first step towards clarity. You turn (in your spirit) to see Him, and when you do, the first thing that happens is the veil is removed. This means that all of the religious filters, agendas, and baggage is removed. The cloud that is over your eyes is evaporated.

Besides that, you cannot give anyone your full attention without physically turning to look at them! Let's say that you are going to have a conversation with one of your friends while sitting in a coffee shop. Your friend is sitting right across from you at the table. When are you going to start your conversation? Are you going to look to the coffee bar which is off to your left? Of course not! You would look directly at your friend who is right in front of you. This is turning. You turn your attention to your friend by physically turning your body to face them. Then, you begin your conversation. When you turn to the Lord, you change your position (mentally and spiritually) to face Him directly. And this turning process requires that you clear your mind, will, and emotions of everything else that isn't Christ. And then, give Him your full attention.

As stated before, every time your mind wanders, gently bring it back to the living Lord inside of you. And again, this will take much practice. But if you will do this during your specially focused time with the Lord every day, then it will become easier to practice this turning to Him all throughout your day.

Chapter Eleven

Seeing Christ in Everyday Things

Turning to our Lord throughout the day is one of the greatest privileges and opportunities that we will ever have. Just think of it. We get to fellowship (and abide in that fellowship) with the Creator of the universe! Not only that, but we get the holy privilege of beholding and abiding in and with Him throughout the rest of eternity! Wow! Pure bliss forever. Folks, I don't think it can get any better than that. So now, let's take a look at some ways and tools that will help us to turn to Him and behold Him throughout the day.

Calling Upon the Name of the Lord

This is a very simple and yet powerful tool to use whenever we remember Him. Simply speak His wonderful name. "Lord Jesus" is one of my favorites. Here are just a few references in the scriptures to this practice:

1 Cor. 1:2: "To the church of God which is at Corinth, to those who have been sanctified in Christ Jesus, saints by calling, with all who in every place *call on the name of our Lord Jesus Christ*, their Lord and ours."

Rom. 10:13: "for whoever will call on the *name of the Lord* will be saved."

Heb. 13:15: "Through Him then, let us continually offer up a sacrifice of praise to God, that is, the fruit of lips that *give thanks to His name.*"

We can call upon His name all throughout the day. Whenever I remember, I will softly and lovingly speak, "Lord Jesus." There is power in that name. And when you speak it to yourself, it serves to bring the center of your being back to the Lord Himself. Now your mind is stayed on Him. You can even whisper His name under your breath when you are with other people. I do it all the time. Don't worry, it's not rude. Remember that you have both a soul and a spirit. Your soul can focus on one thing while your spirit is focusing on the Lord. It may sound crazy, but it's totally true. When you go about your daily chores you can focus on what you are doing and yet still focus on the Christ who lives within. The chores are being done with your soul (mind, will, emotions) and your worship is being done with your spirit. Yes, you truly can do two things at the same time!

That's one of the beautiful benefits of learning to call upon the name of the Lord. Just by speaking His name, your spirit will respond. It may just be a spark...but there you have it, eternal life! God's life. Divine life. And that's the goal of the Holy Spirit within us—for His life to be expressed through us. You see, the more you learn to practice this (and other things throughout this book), the more the life of

Christ will be displayed through you and the more God will accomplish His eternal purpose through you.

Please be aware, however, that speaking or calling upon the name of the Lord is not some mantra or magical phrase. You could call it a trigger, though. It's a way for your soul to remind your spirit to turn to Christ within. When you speak His name, your spirit responds in a very loving way to the Lord. In other words...worship! Let me take a minute to explain that word to you according to what the Lord Jesus said to the woman at the well.

> Jesus said to her, "Woman, believe Me, an hour is coming when neither in this mountain nor in Jerusalem will you worship the Father. You worship what you do not know; we worship what we know, for salvation is from the Jews. But an hour is coming, and now is, when the true worshipers will worship the Father in spirit and truth; for such people the Father seeks to be His worshipers. God is spirit, and those who worship Him must worship in spirit and truth" (John 4:21-24).

The Greek word for "worship" here is *proskuneo*, which literally means "to move towards a kiss." Yes! This word means to kiss the living God (spiritually speaking, of course). It's a romantic word. It means to partake in this divine romance between the bridegroom and his bride. Dear saint, you are a part of the bride, and your bridegroom wishes to know you intimately in the most holy of ways possible. So, when we call upon the name of our Lord, we are calling Him so we can have intimate fellowship with the living God. And we can do this at any time throughout the day.

Seeing Christ in Nature

> For since the creation of the world, His invisible attributes, His eternal power and divine nature, have been clearly seen, being understood through what has been made, so that they are without excuse (Rom. 1:20).

We know that our God is the God of all creation; visible and invisible. He is the Creator. In this verse in Romans chapter one, Paul is telling us that God's eternal power and divine nature have been seen in what He has made. In other words, in His creation. We can use the creation (or nature) as a trigger to turn to Him and behold Him.

As I have shared previously in this book, our Lord referred to Himself in many ways. One of the ways was through a grape vine. He said, "I am the *true* (real or genuine) vine and you are the branches." He said this as He was walking through a vineyard with His disciples. What He was doing was seeing His Father's eternal purpose in nature.

Another way of saying and seeing this is something Paul said later: "He is the head and we are the body." God's purpose is to have a vine or to have a new man. He is the vine and we are the branches. Or He is the head and we are the body. This is "seeing" Christ in nature. From now on you will never see a grapevine the same! You will never see the human body the same! Christ and the church will come to mind whenever you see these things. This, my friends, is beholding Christ in that which has been created.

We must understand that the Father Creator is totally focused on His Son. Do you honestly think that the Father could ever create anything without beholding the Son? No way. Impossible. Never happen! So, if the Father had Christ in mind when He created do you think that it's possible for us to have Christ in mind when we view this creation? Absolutely! Can you see Him in a bird? In a tree? In a mountain or a stream? Can you see Him in a leaf? Can you see Him in a tiny bug?

When I was a young boy of about twelve years, our school class went up to the mountains in San Bernadino, California, to a camp for a week. It really impacted my life because our camp counselor took us on nature walks. He would lead us on trails through the woods and teach us how to really see all the beauty around us and appreciate it. Even though this was not a spiritual retreat, I learned to appreciate God's creation that week. Ever since, I have loved to take nature walks and be with and behold my Lord in His creation. My wife and I now live in a very beautiful place in Western Colorado and I still love to take those nature walks and behold my Lord in the beauty around me.

This is not difficult to do once you get the hang of it. For example, you can take hold of the branch of a tree and take a new look at it. See how the thickness of the branch gets thinner and thinner as it approaches the leaves. And then see the leaf itself. See the veins within the leaf. It's almost as if the tiny veins within the leaf is an extension of the branch itself and the branch itself is an extension of the trunk. How does this remind you of your Lord? Can you see Him as the root, the trunk, and the branch (Father, Son, Spirit)? Can you see the leaves as all the members of the body of Christ? How does the life of God flow through that tree? As you can see, this one example can be quite a deep revelation and beholding of Christ within you. You can spend some wonderful time with the Lord beholding Him as the true (real) Tree!

And what about a stream? Or the cool breeze? Or the mountain itself? Or an ant hill? Or a young doe?

Francis of Assisi was a brother who understood how to see Christ in the beauty of nature around us. I highly recommend a movie about his life called *Brother Son Sister Moon.*

Why not take a walk with the Lord today? You don't have to live in the mountains of Colorado to do this. Why not head over to a park and spend some time beholding Him in the grass and the trees? Or to the beach? Or just walk out to your own backyard!

Seeing Christ in His Body

Can you see (behold) the Lord in your brothers and sisters in Christ? Yes! If you are looking for Him. All those who have been born from above are a part of the corporate Christ.

> For even as the body is one and yet has many members, and all the members of the body, though they are many, are one body, so also is Christ. For by one Spirit we were all baptized into one body, whether Jews or Greeks, whether slaves or free, and we were all made to drink of one Spirit. For the body is not one member, but many (1 Cor. 12:12-14).

This is a most incredible portion of scripture. Paul is telling us that the body has many members and yet there is only one body. He is comparing the church to the human body, but then He does something even more incredible. He says that the body is Christ: "...though they are many, are one body, so also is Christ."

Did you get that? The one body *is* Christ! Please let that sink in for a moment. The head (Jesus Christ) and the body (His people) make up the one Christ.

Do you consider your fellow members of the body as members of the living Christ? If we really had this revelation, then we would most likely treat our brothers and sisters completely different. If we would get this understanding, then it would not be difficult to behold the Lord in our brothers in sisters.

Then why is it difficult sometimes? It's because we are *beholding* the flesh. What I mean by that is when our brother or sister in Christ is acting or speaking in a way that seems out of line with the nature of Christ, then we tend to judge them according to our own flesh. Hey, we all still have the flesh nature in us, and it does manifest itself at times. Isn't that true in your own life? The problem is that the flesh activates the flesh. When you experience the flesh in another believer then it activates the flesh inside of you and then you react in a not-so-Christ-like manner! This is simply Newton's third law of action and reaction applied spiritually (or should I say *fleshly*?).

What is the solution to this dilemma? The only solution that I know of is called *transformation*. As we behold the Lord, we are being transformed from glory to glory into His own image. Christ-like character can never come out of the fallen flesh. It can only come out from the Spirit who lives within you and is changing you into a Christ-person. Any attempts at changing our character and behavior that come from ourselves is called *religion*. This is the fallen flesh trying to be spiritual. It can never happen! The gifts and fruit of the Holy Spirit can only come about by and through transformation. And this transfiguration only comes about by the cross being applied to our old man and the spirit being activated by beholding Him.

So, the more you learn to behold Christ and allow Him to crucify that old man, the more your mind, will, and emotions change towards the body of Christ. You will find yourself loving the saints like never before. Even though they might irritate you from time to time, something is changing inside of you, and you find yourself overlooking things and loving them despite the faults.

Seeing Christ in Your Circumstances

> What we need is this seeing of the exalted Lord and His glory;
> and this seeing is essential to our salvation, not only as believ-
> ers in God, but for those of us who are Christian workers, in
> order to get us through. If we have not seen the significance
> and the meaning of the Man in the Throne, we shall just go to
> pieces under the duress of disillusionment and disappointment.
> -T. Austin-Sparks

It's so easy to see our precious Lord in those circumstances that we deem to be positive. For example, I just got "blessed" by receiving a bunch of money that I didn't expect. Wow! God really "blessed" me. "Thank you, Lord!" But do we say those things when something happens we deem to be negative? When someone hurts us? Or when we lose? Or when we are rejected or ridiculed? Can we see the Lord in those circumstances?

"And we know that God causes all things to work together for good to those who love God, to those who are called according to His purpose" (Romans 8:28). Do you love God? Are you called according to his purpose? If you answered yes to these two questions, then all your circumstances are working together for good—even if it doesn't look that way. Just think about the life of the man who wrote these words (Paul). Talk about trials and tribulations! Talk about persecution! Talk about a hard life! And yet he could see Christ in all of these circumstances. Paul was a brother who knew his identity in Christ. He knew that he was a member of the body of Christ. He knew that he was one with the living Lord. He knew that he was a *sent one* (apostle) of Christ. He knew that Christ was his all in all. He knew that God lived inside of Him and that he lived inside of the living God. He knew, he knew, he knew. And because he knew, he had the confidence to be all that he was inside of Christ. Because he knew, he had the confidence to do the work to which God had called Him. Because he knew, he could go out boldly doing the exploits of his God. You see, despite all of the negative circumstances and the opposition...he knew!

How about you dear believer? Do you know who you are in Christ? Do you have all the confidence in He who has called you out of darkness and into his marvelous light? It will take that kind of confidence and faith to overcome difficult circumstances. But here is the most important truth: You are already an overcomer because the overcomer lives inside of you! He is our victory!

Seeing Christ in Art and the Media

Can you really behold Christ in art and the media? Is it possible? Before I answer that question let me explain a few very important things first.

- **Christ lives in you.** Jesus Christ (by His Spirit) literally and spiritually actually lives inside of you! This point has almost been totally lost in many Christian circles today, and yet it is extremely important for you to understand in order to learn how to fellowship with Him on a daily basis. The scriptures make this very clear by what the Lord Himself taught and what Paul wrote especially in letters such as Colossians and Ephesians. This must become more than just a theory or a doctrine for you. It must become your very life!
- **You live in Christ.** This is an equally and vitally important truth. It is a spiritual reality. It is fact. You are actually inside of Jesus Christ right now as you read these words! Do you believe that? I hope so, because your daily life with the

Lord depends upon it. What is your place of residence? Jesus Christ. That is happening now and forever more. You may not be aware of that fact all of the time, but it is true, nonetheless. You may not be abiding in that reality all of the time, but it exists still. The key now is to learn how to be aware and to abide in that wonderful reality that you are actually inside of your Lord twenty-four seven.

You may be wondering, "Milt, what in the world does this have to do with seeing Christ in art and the media?" Well, it has everything to do with it. Let me explain it from a media example. I have been a fan of Jerry Seinfeld and his TV show that was on years ago. No, I didn't care for everything that was said and done on that show, but I want to share a particular episode in which I really saw the Lord. It was the episode about the "bubble boy." These older folks had a grown son that had a disease that made him very vulnerable to many contagions. For this reason, he had to live in a big plastic bubble the size of a small room. He could not leave the bubble, or he would catch some disease and die. His whole life was lived out inside of this bubble environment. On the Seinfeld show this was used as a situational comedy routine, but this is a picture of how we live inside of Christ. Another similar example is the space suits that the astronauts wear. All of their environment is controlled by and in the suit. Their oxygen, food, waste, are all taken care of inside of this suit. Christ is your environment. Everything you do and everything you need is inside of this environment. So now, maybe you are starting to get the picture.

For He rescued us from the domain of darkness, and transferred us to the kingdom of His beloved Son, in whom we have redemption, the forgiveness of sins (Col. 1:13-14).

He is before all things, and **in Him** all things hold together (Col. 1:17).

For it was the Father's good pleasure for all the fullness to dwell **in Him** (Col. 1:19).

We proclaim Him, admonishing every man and teaching every man with all wisdom, so that we may present every man complete **in Christ** (Col. 1:28).

So, if Christ is your environment (and He is) then that means when you look at anything in this existence, we are looking through the filter of Christ! Imagine yourself inside of a physical bubble. When you look at anything in the world you are looking *through* the environment within the bubble. You, dear believer, are inside of Christ right now. If you have eyes to see, then you can view the things around you from the perspective of Christ because He is your "first-stage environment." If you can, picture in your mind a circle within a circle. The inner circle is you. The circle that you are in is Christ. This circle within a circle is in the world. Since you are within Christ, when you look at the world, you are looking through the "atmosphere" of Christ. Now, you can either look through Christ in a nebulous way, or you can pick up hints of Christ as you look through Him into the world. This is beholding Christ in the world around you.

Now, of course, we must be careful here because the world is a fallen and sinful place. You cannot see Christ in everything in the world. For example, crime, sexual perversion, violence, murder (and so on) are not a part of our Lord. Therefore, there are many aspects of art and the media where you just cannot behold the Lord. Because of the fall, there is much mixture in everything, and you will need to use your God-given discernment. For example, in one movie, I might be able to see Christ in one part and not the other. This is quite common. Of course, some Christians have a sin filter on all the time. All they can see is sin all over the place. But my question is: What are you looking for? If you are looking for sin (being sin-focused), then you will find it everywhere. But if you are looking for Christ (being Christ-focused), then you will find Him everywhere. Beholding sin will not transform you. Only beholding Christ will change you into His image from glory to glory!

Yes, you can see Christ in art, music, and the movies. Sometimes it's very easy and sometimes it is not. It's extremely easy to behold the Lord in Handel's Messiah. Wow! What a masterpiece. I don't know if Handel was a born-again believer or not, but God definitely used him to write that piece of music. And yet, other pieces of music seem to have none of the Lord in them at all (at least from my perspective). We also have to realize that the arts and media can be very subjective. A song in which one person sees Christ may not be so for another. I think the rule of thumb here is always to go with the life of the Lord. If you sense His life within it, then go for it. I really love music and movies. Some of my favorites in which to see Christ are *The Matrix*, *The Notebook*, *The Greatest Showman*, *Lady in the Water*, *Signs*, and many others. (I suggest mentioning a movie list that you add to the end of the book after the recommended reading instead of listing them here.)

Remember, you can see Him everywhere...if you are looking for Him.

Seeing Christ Together

Seeing the Lord together with other saints (believers) is an extremely important facet of beholding the Lord. It's actually the backbone and foundation for the life of the church. Without brothers and sisters beholding the Lord together, the church will become something quite different than the Lord's intention. It will become an organization based upon rules and regulations inside of His life. It will be something, not Someone. It will be a religion of man rather than the corporate life of Christ being expressed in the world.

Suffice it to say that this is a huge topic all within itself. Since beholding the Lord together with other saints is so important to the ongoing life of the church, I have dedicated part three of this book to that very subject so that we can go into it in much more detail.

Part two of this book was all about learning to see (behold) Christ as your all. I was going to write that beholding Christ should become "second nature" to you, but that's not quite right. It should become "first nature" to you! And this takes practice. But if you are learning to behold Him in the beginning of your day, and then throughout your day, and then every day, this will become easier and easier. Believe me. It's true.

PART THREE

Beholding Christ Together

*But **we all** with **our** face having been unveiled, having beheld the glory of the Lord in a mirror, are being changed into the same image from glory to glory, as from the Lord Spirit (*
2 Cor. 3:16).

In it I became a minister in accordance with the divine steward-ship which was entrusted to me for you (plural) [as its object and for your benefit], to make the Word of God fully known [among you]—the mystery of which was hidden for ages and generations [from angels and men], but is now revealed to His holy people (the saints), To whom God was pleased to make known how great for the Gentiles are the riches of the glory of this mystery, which is Christ within and among you (plural), the Hope of [realizing the] glory. Him we preach and proclaim, warning and admonishing everyone and instructing everyone in all wisdom (comprehensive insight into the ways and purposes of God), that we may present every person mature (full-grown, fully initiated, complete, and perfect) in Christ (the Anointed One) (Col. 1:25-28).

*He made known to **us** the mystery of His will, according to His kind intention which He purposed in Him with a view to an administration suitable to the fullness of the times, that is, the summing up of all things in Christ, things in the heavens and things on the earth. In Him also **we** have obtained an inheritance, having been predestined according to His purpose who works all things after the counsel of His will, to the end that **we** who were the first to hope in Christ would be to the praise of His glory* (Eph. 1:9-12).

*Therefore, since **we** have so great a cloud of witnesses surrounding **us**, let **us** also lay aside every encumbrance and the sin which so easily entangles **us**, and let **us** run with endurance the race that is set before **us**, fixing **our** eyes on Jesus, the author and perfecter of faith, who for the joy set before Him endured the cross, despising the shame, and has sat down at the right hand of the throne of God* (Heb. 12:1-2).

If eyes have been opened; if, in any sense—not officially—you have become a "seer"—one who sees: it is going to cost you a lot, it will involve you in a lot of trouble. This matter of "seeing" does that. It was Elijah the Seer, over against the blindness of Israel. It is a costly thing to be a spiritual man or a spiritual woman in this universe. It is a costly thing, yes, very costly, to hold to a heavenly and spiritual position. It is a costly thing to hold for Christ's full place; it involves you in trouble. It is a costly thing to have light—if it is true light, God-given light. It is a costly thing to have Life. But remember, it is here, in this, that the power is resident.

T. Austin-Sparks

Chapter Twelve

The Purpose of the Church

One thing that we definitely need to understand is that beholding the Lord is not only for the individual believer but also most definitely for the church.

"But we all with our face having been unveiled, having beheld the glory of the Lord as in a mirror, are being changed into the same image from glory to glory as from the Lord Spirit." 2 Cor. 3:16

The Image of God

God's eternal purpose is all about Him getting His image displayed throughout all of creation... visible and invisible.

This is the "purpose" or reason why He created heaven and earth; the visible and invisible realms. Of course, Jesus prayed for this purpose when He prayed: "Your kingdom come, Your will be done, on earth as it is in heaven." So... the purpose is to have God's kingdom (rule) in all realms.

In order to accomplish this purpose, God needs to have an expression or "image" of Himself. This is to prove and display to all of creation that He is a loving and kind God. But He is also a mighty and powerful God who will execute justice when needed in all realms. Since He is the Creator He has full rights to execute justice when needed.

The concept of "image" is all about expression. God very much wants to show or "express" Himself in all of His creation. This is why He created "Man". The human race was created by God to be His expression or image. God very much wants to be known. He wants to share all that He is and does with humans.

This is why He created us in His image. It's so that we would be able to relate to Him and understand Him. Of course, God is Spirit and those who know (understand and relate to Him), must be able to do so in Spirit. That is why He created us to have a human spirit and could receive God's Spirit. But, of course, this is a matter of freedom of choice. God never forces us to receive Himself.

The Snare of Individualism

We live in a very separate and individualistic world. The question often arises, *"why can't we all just get along with one another?"* Of course, the answer is *"the fall of Man."* The opposite of oneness is separation. Our God is all about oneness. He is one God in three Persons (Father, Son, and Spirit). So, of course, His image (expression) be many who are One. But, as we all know, there was an angel who rebelled against this oneness (community) who wanted to be the highest one above all others. His name was Lucifer. He was a very beautiful archangel who wanted to rise above all others (even the throne of God!) But, guess what? God had a plan!

<u>The Incarnation</u>

How did the almighty God conquer the evil one... Satan? How did God conquer the devil and all of his fallen angels? Was it by God Himself gathering together a bigger and stronger army than Lucifer? Was it by God stretching out His mighty hand to smite and defeat all disobedience and rebellion and sin?

How did the Lion of Judah defeat all evil? How did the Creator of all things conquer death? How did the Lord God stop all of the madness?

How did He do it?

By the Lion of Judah becoming a little, weak, innocent, and broken Lamb!

By that Lamb being slaughtered on a cross of wood!

Just think... He who is the greatest of all became the least of all!

And because of this HE became a many membered Christ!

One thing that we definitely need to understand is that beholding the Lord is not only for the individual believer, but also most definitely for the church.

> "But **we all** with **our** face having been unveiled, having beheld the glory of the Lord in a mirror, are being changed into the same image from glory to glory, as from the Lord Spirit (2 Cor. 3:16).

As we can see from this scripture, this beholding thing is definitely something that *we all* do together. That's because it's not only that *we all* behold but it's because *we all* are being transformed together into His image.

Transformation is a corporate thing. It's a *we all* thing. Therefore, beholding is a *we all* thing.

Beholding brings us to transformation and transformation brings us to the eternal purpose of God. And the eternal purpose of God is that we would be transformed (changed) into His image. As I shared in chapters two and four, this idea of "image" is a very important one in the scriptures. Let's take a quick look at that, again.

> Then God said, "Let Us make mankind in Our image, according to Our likeness; and let them rule over the fish of the sea and over the birds of the sky and over the cattle and over all the earth, and over every creeping thing that creeps on the earth (Gen. 1:26).

Mankind was created to exist in the image of God, and that the image was corporate. A corporate God (Father, Son, Spirit) wanted a corporate image. This corporate image (the race of mankind) was to rule over God's creation.

"God created man in His own image, in the image of God He created him; male and female He created them" (Gen. 1:27). This image was to include two parts—the male and the female.

"That is why a man will leave his father and mother and be united with his wife, and the two will become one flesh. This is a great secret, but I am talking about Christ and the church" (Eph. 5:31-32).

Paul said this is a great secret or mystery—Christ and the church. So, there is a head and a body; a bridegroom and a bride. And they are one. And together they make up the *image* of God. The image is Christ *and* the church. The image is a *corporate* image. And we can also see this from Paul's writings in 1 Corinthians 12

"For just as the body is one and yet has many parts, and all the parts of the body, though many, form one body, so it is with Christ." (1 Corinthians 12:12)

Please notice that Paul calls the body Christ. He doesn't say that the body is *like Christ*. He clearly states that the body *is* Christ. We are talking about a corporate person here. Of course, that person is nonfunctional without the head. But the fact still remains that all of the body parts are members of the living Christ. (This, of course, is extremely important to remember when you consider how you are treating your brothers and sisters in Christ.)

I have shared this before, but it is worth repeating: God wants to have an image, an expression, of Himself. This is described in many different ways in the scriptures. This image is also called the body, the bride, the house, the city, the sheep, the new man, the new creation, the new race, the vine and branches, the new Jerusalem, the church, the eternal purpose, and so much more. The purpose of this image is to display the glories of our Christ to all of creation, both visible and invisible!

As I explained in part two, this is why beholding Him is so vital to God's eternal purpose. When we behold Him then we are being transformed into His image. And when we are transformed into that image then all of creation can see Him and know Him. When I say *know Him*, I am not just referring to being saved or born-again. That is just the beginning. I am talking about knowing this Christ in the most intimate sense of the word. Knowing Him deeply. Knowing Him intimately. Knowing Him in a much greater way than you have ever known anyone. Our God wants to be known. He wants to be known deeply and intimately. And He wants to be known in that way by a beautiful woman that He calls His Bride.

It's only when you have known someone deeply that you can express their life. God wants His life to be experienced by His church and to be expressed through His church. Therefore, it's very important indeed that we, as His body, learn to behold Him *individually* and *together*. Now let's take a look at some of the ways that we can behold Him together.

Chapter Thirteen

Corporate Beholding

When most believers think about their devotional lives they think about private prayer, Bible reading, worship, etc. It's typically a very private matter—between you and Jesus. Of course, as I have discussed earlier in this book, there definitely is a private aspect to fellowshipping or beholding the Lord. However, this is only one aspect of this beautiful practice. When other believers are added to the equation a whole new dimension opens up.

To be clear, I am not referring to "prayer meetings." Those are good and needed at particular times in the life of a church. We can read about such a time in the life of the early church in Acts 12. Peter had been in prison but the angel of the Lord released him. He immediately went to the house of Mary where there was a group of believers praying for Peter. This is an example of a prayer meeting of the church that was called for a specific reason: the release of Peter from prision. Please understand that I am not referring to this sort of meeting.

Rather, I am referring to a gathering of believers for the sole purpose of beholding the Lord. Or, at least, it may begin that way. When you start out by seeing and loving the Lord in your gathering, then this releases Him to lead the group into all kinds of things. You are not coming with an agenda per se. You are only gathering for the purpose of seeking the mind of Christ together for His kingdom on the earth. You begin by everyone present turning to the Lord who lives inside of them. Usually this will begin with a quiet time of beholding and centering your spirit, soul, and mind on Christ alone. As you do this quietly, you will find that He will begin to speak to you and to the other saints around you. Perhaps it will begin with certain ones speaking words of praise, love, and adoration to the Lord. Then some may have words of exhortation or a call to action for the group. Some of these words can be predictive or prophetic in the sense of something the Lord is going to do in the future. Whatever happens is a direct result of having spent time with Jesus. You don't start out with prayer (i.e. asking for things), you don't start out with Bible study, and you don't start out with any agenda other than to fellowship with the living Christ within you! Everything else comes out of that. Everything else is a fruit of beholding Him and knowing Him. This is extremely important.

Just as I recommended that you start your private time with the Lord, so I suggest that you start your corporate time with Him in a similar fashion. All spiritual things come from God Himself through His Son Jesus Christ. Just as He said that He was the vine and we are the branches, so the only way that any lasting fruit can be produced is by abiding (remaining, living) in Him. Whoever heard of a branch jumping off of the vine every other minute to live by it's own life?

It seems like most of us are come-and-go Christians who have our "prayer time," "worship time." "fellowship time," and "Bible reading time," and yet, where is the constant abiding with and in Him? There must be a way to do this or our Lord would not have told us to abide in Him. The main purpose for a local fellowship of believers is this very thing.

Yes, we are called to be the light of the world and the salt of the earth. But my brothers and sisters, we cannot be those things unless we learn to live (abide) by His life together! The whole context for the Lord's words in John 15 about the vine and the branches is the corporate life. Have you ever been to a vineyard and seen the vines? If not, I recommend that you do so sometime. The vines are one. In fact, it is very difficult to distinguish the branches from the vine. It all flows together.

What I am attempting to describe here is very rare in the church today. This is unfortunate, yet the Lord is bringing His true expression back to this planet and you can be a part of it! He has always kept a witness or testimony of His church down through the ages and you can trace that if you read such books as *The Torch of the Testimony* by John W. Kennedy and *The Pilgrim Church* by E.H. Broadbent.

Addendum

We have been so individualized (is that a word?) in this world system that we think this way (individually) is the best and most logical way to do things. And to think, and reason, and build our lives, and build society all with the individual in mind is the way to do it.

In the rest of the final part of this book, I will be sharing with you some of the things that I have learned from my experiences in the church of Jesus Christ regarding knowing and abiding in that beautiful and glorious vine.

Chapter Fourteen

Partnering Together

"For where two or three have gathered together in My name, I am there in their midst" (Matt. 18:20).

This is a wonderful promise that our Lord gives us, but please notice with me that there is a condition to this promise: *in My name.* It's only as two or three gather *in His name* that He promises to be in our midst. It's crucially important that we understand what these three words actually mean.

The Name

Gathering together *in His name* does not mean that we begin with a prayer saying, "We are now gathering in the name of Jesus." Just saying "in the name of Jesus" does not mean anything. In the first century, when a king would send a servant *in his name* to another country, this meant that the servant came to those folks with the same power and authority as the king. It was just as if the king was going to them himself! *In the name* meant *in the person*. The name and the person were synonomous. The meaning of *in My name* has nothing to do with just simply saying the phrase "in the name of Jesus." This has been missused by believers for centuries. We think that if we tack "in the name of Jesus" onto our prayers that the Lord has to hear us. Nonsense! God only hears His Son. If we do not approach Him with and in His Son, then He cannot receive us. Does this make sense to you? But if we come *in* and *as* the body of the living Christ, then that is a totally differnt matter to God. Part of that means knowing who we are in Christ. Many believers today have no idea of their identity in Christ. For this reason I have written a whole book on this topic entitled *The Butterfly in You*.

When we have gathered with one or two other believers (saints, holy ones), then we come with an awareness that we are approaching a holy God and entering into His holy presence. But we also know (by revelation) that we are part of this Christ and we are in this Christ and we share in that holiness, power, and life. We don't gather together in our power, life, or strength, we gather together *in Christ*.

How to Begin

The Sound of Silence

We begin together the same way that we begin alone: by quietly beholding our glorious Lord. We center all of our minds, wills, and emotions upon Him. We "turn our eyes upon Jesus and look full into his wonderful face." We get lost in His glory. We get impassioned by His love. We get focused by His eternal purpose. We sit quietly in His presence and just look at Him and love Him. And when our hearts are full of his love, then we speak those words of love back to Him. We open our mouths and then let the living Christ come out!

Now please be aware that when you are doing this with other saints that you are not alone. Be sensitive to giving room for others to speak words of love to the Lord as well. In others words, don't hog the time together! This is not just about you. This is about your Lord first and His bride second. The beautiful thing is that you can not only speak to your Lord, but you can also listen to your brothers and sisters speak to Him. As you hear their words of praise and adoration, it will spark something in your spirit to speak softly and gently words of agreement and appreciation for what your Lord is giving them as well. This is an incredibly beautiful aspect that can only be experienced in this corporate time with the Lord.

Remember that your spirit is one with their spirits. And you are all one with His Spirit. Don't just be anxious to speak something in this gathering, but rather be poised to listen to what the Lord is speaking through your brothers and sisters. And then, if appropriate, add your contribution to theirs. Be slow to speak but quick to listen. Remember that this is a conversation. A conversation between the Lord of the universe and His bride.

Please do not make the mistake of comparing yourself to others in your gathering. Their expression of the Lord will be different from yours, but that's the way it's supposed to be. Christ expresses Himself differently through all of His members in the body. He created us that way so that He would have a many-membered body that would express Him in His fullness!

What I am sharing here comes from a place of experience. It applies to all gatherings of the saints whether there are two present or two hundred. Some of the most precious times I have had with other saints was in times of silence to the Lord. I remember one specific meeting in which a brother had been invited who was not accustomed to these types of gatherings. We went for about fifteen minutes without a word and then this brother could not stand it any longer and spoke out loudly with, "What kind of prayer meeting is this?" We all just looked at one another and smiled and one of the brothers said, "Well, up to this time, apparently, it is a quiet one!"

> My soul, wait in silence for God only, for my hope is from Him (Psalms 62:5).

As I discussed in part two, in our noisy and fast-paced life, it seems that silence is a rare thing. Busyness and noise seem to permeate everything. We desperately need to quite our souls (minds, wills, and emotions) so that we can get down to something much deeper...our spirits! However, this is not easy and many will fall by the wayside in their attempts. But I would encourage you, dear reader, to press in and press on, together! Allow your mind, will, and emotions to rest and be quiet. And out of the silence...God will speak.

He will speak through your brothers and sisters and, oh, yes, He will speak through you! And it won't be just a bunch of religious garbage. And it won't be just a bunch of rhetoric. But it will be life! His life! And you will all be edified.

Beholding Christ in the Scriptures

In the last part of this book, I described beholding Christ in the scriptures. However, now I would like to share how this differs when you are partnering with others.

This practice can be referred to as "beholding Christ in the scriptures," "praying the scriptures," or "devotional scripture reading." It's actually an ancient practice and many of those whom I have already mentioned in this book have practiced it throughout the ages. People such as Brother Lawrence, Jeanne Guyon, Frank Laubach, Francois Fenelon, and many more have written about this practice.

When we approach the Lord in this way it is a time for beholding, loving, and communicating, which is different than studying the scriptures. Although it can be called "praying" the scriptures, the problem with this word is that many have the idea that prayer is only interceding or asking God for things. This is not true. Prayer is also fellowship with God. So, this time in the scriptures is not about study (an intellectual exercise) and its not about asking God for things for yourself or for others. Rather it's about enjoying, loving, abiding, and beholding Him. When you get together with your partner(s), you are not going to *discuss* the Bible. You are not going to take a portion of scripture, look it up in your Bible dictionary or concordance and then figure out the meaning. You are not going to discuss the Greek or Hebrew words and their meanings. You are not going to do an exegesis of the text. You are simply going to use God's word to fellowship with Him.

I realize that this practice may be totally foreign to many of you. That's okay. Probably most of the practices in this book are anyway! So don't be afraid to venture onward. Especially some of my more "fundamentalist" friends out there. If you are willing to take this step of faith, I am sure that you will discover a whole new world available to you inside of your precious Lord.

Now on to some practical advice and examples:
(Note: I strongly suggest that partner groups be restricted to either married couples or same-gender partners. Having a brother and a sister (who are not married) meeting together privately is not a wise practice. You might be thinking that this goes without saying, but believe me, it needs to be said in our day and age!)

Psalm 23: Take this well-known psalm and turn it into prayer/ praise with a partner.

- Since this psalm is so short, I recommend that one person read the whole psalm out loud and slowly. Then both of you spend some time quietly before your great shepherd.
- As you feel prompted by the Spirit, each one of you begin to share your words of love and appreciation for your Lord as your shepherd. Please do not speak in a "stained-glass" voice. Speak normally as you would when you are speaking to your spouse or a good friend. Here is a short example of what one might say to the Lord: "Lord Jesus, you are my beautiful shepherd. There is no greater experience in my life than knowing and following You. I have everything I need because I have You! I am lacking nothing. You are my all. You are my everything. What an all-loving and all-inclusive shepherd you are! I love you, Lord. Not just because of what you give me but also because of who you are." (And this is just taken from verse 1.)
- Now there are different ways to do this, such as taking alternate verses. One partner can take verse one and the other partner take verse two, and so on. This could be a possible version for the second partner for verse two: "Lord you always provide for me the perfect environment for our fellowship. Sometimes I don't really like the environment you have provided and yet it always feeds me and waters me. That's because even from within what I see as a 'negative' environment, you reveal yourself to me in a greater way. That is my portion. That is my food and drink. It is just you Lord! Thank you for providing the place and the nourishment."

- And then the other partner would take verse three and so on, alternating verses as you go. Remember that this is just one way to do this. Don't be afraid to get creative and come up with your own ways to behold the Lord in scripture.

Now please understand that this is not a competition. You are not here to try and "out do" one another. This is a holy place and time. Just keep it simple and from your heart. Don't worry about how what you are saying sounds like to your partner. You are saying this to your Lord! And what He cares about is that you are saying it from your heart with love for Him. That's all.

Now, let's take another totally different approach to using Psalm 23 to turn to the Lord together.

What if you could see this awesome psalm from a totally new perspective? What if you could look into the Godhead Himself and see this psalm? Hopefully you believe that God is three Persons (Father, Son, and Spirit) who are one. (For more on this I would suggest my book "The Community Life of God.") And what about the church? Is she involved in all of this fellowship? Of course! Remember, this isn't just an individual thing, it's also a corporate or community thing. And all community comes from God Himself. He is the community. So now let's take another approach and take a look at another example.

Psalm 23: Considered from the perspective of the Father, Son, and Spirit.

Read verses 3-5 and speak it from the perspective of the Son speaking to the Father:

- "Father, you build me up and edify my soul. You lead me in your pathways for your glory."

- "Even though daily I am walking in an attitude of death to myself and my own selfishness and self centeredness and self interests, a very dark place to be indeed. And yet, I have no need to worry or fret because in all of this…You are with and in me! You strengthen me with your correction and discipline."
- "In fact, you even setup a banquet in the midst of all this! Father, you and I can have fellowship constantly even in the midst of all this suffering in this world. I love you Father! You give me the anointing of your Spirit and fill me to overflowing!"

Now, we can reverse it and speak from the perspective of the Father speaking to the Son in verse six.

- "My Son, I want you to know that my friends, mercy and goodness, will be in you and with you all of the days of your life. And you, my precious Son, will abide forever in my House. In fact, I have made you to be my house! And inside of that house will live all of my sons and daughters forever!"

A really cool way to do this is to have three partners speak this psalm to the Lord and one another out loud as the voices of the Godhead. Now, at first, this may sound very odd to you. You may be thinking, "Milt, really! You are asking us to pray and speak in the voice of God?" Well…yes, I am. "But isn't that blasphemous?" No it isn't. Actually the Bible has a name for this and it's called *prophecy*. This is a prophetic practice. In the Bible, we see that many men and women down through the centuries spoke for God. They were actually used of the Spirit to speak God's words. But, of course, if you are uncomfortable with this particular aspect of beholding the Lord in scripture then you certainly are free to bow out. However, from my own experience, this has been one of the most glorious and rewarding ways to fellowship with the Lord with other believers.

What if you were sitting in a living room with about fifteen other saints and they all (one by one) began to share these things? What if a whole group did this? (That is, took Psalm 23 and spoke it in the voices of the Father, Son, and Spirit.) I have personally been in meetings like this and I can attest to the fact that they were glorious! I will never forget those meetings as long as I live. It's as if the Trinity was right there speaking to all of us. And, of course, He was! Since the Godhead was residing in everyone there, He spoke through them and to them.

Now, I would not attempt this with a group that was not first practiced in beholding the Lord as individuals first. The believers involved need to first have a foundation of "seeing" Christ as I have been describing in this book. I'm not saying that it can't happen without that foundation, but I believe that it will happen with more intensity and power when there is a group who is practiced in the art of beholding.

Beholding Christ through Singing and Speaking Songs

...speaking to one another in psalms and hymns and spiritual songs, singing and making melody with your heart to the Lord (Eph. 5:19).

Notice there are several things shared in this verse. First of all, it says that we can "speak" to one another in psalms, hymns, and spiritual songs. Interesting. Have you ever thought of speaking songs to your brothers and sisters in Christ? Not singing, but speaking. Yes, we can take the words of the songs and speak them to one another. Wow...so simple...and yet, how many times have you done this? Believe me, just this one simple thing can be extremely powerful in a gathering of believers. When you speak the words of the song, it can now become an exortation, an encouragement, or an instruction. It takes on a whole new flavor when you speak the words to one another. If it's a worship song, then you will be speaking the words to the Lord in the presence of the gathering. This is also very powerful because everyone will now be inspired to agree with you and join in with you in those words of praise and worship.

Secondly, Paul states in this verse that we are to speak and sing songs to one another. Not only to the Lord, but also *to one another*: "Speaking to one another...and singing with your heart to the Lord." So, the early church not only sang songs, but also spoke songs to one another and to the Lord. Have you ever done that in your group? If not, then you are missing quite a bit. Let me give you some examples of this practice.

Scenario #1

You walk into a living room filled with believers who all love the Lord Jesus. They are all chatting. In the midst of this someone in the room starts a song.

> *"You are beautiful beyond description,*
> *Too marvelous for words,"*
> (more people join in the singing)
> *"Too wonderful for comprehension,*
> *Like nothing ever seen or heard,"*
> (more join in)
> *"Who can grasp Your infinite wisdom?*

Who can fathom the depths of Your love?
You are beautiful beyond description,
Majesty enthroned above,
And we stand, we stand in awe of You,"
(at this point everyone stands up)
"We stand, we stand in awe of You,
Mighty God to whom all praise is due,
We stand in awe of You."

The rest of the song is sung and then someone speaks out these words: "Lord Jesus, You are so beautiful! Nothing can compare with You!" Someone else speaks out these words: "Lord we stand in You because we live and breath and have our being inside of You!" Other voices are now beginning to chime in with words of agreement such as "Yes!" and "Amen!" Now, people from all over the room are thanking and praising the Lord. Someone else then starts another song simply by singing it or speaking it.

What is happening here? The body is all functioning in the praise and worship. It's not just one "worship leader" starting the songs. It's the whole church leading the worship. This is tremendous! This is a whole different animal from the typical church "service" where a worship leader leads the singing, the pastor does the preaching, and the deacons take the offering. This is the whole church coming alive. It's every-member-functioning as the apostle Paul talks about.

But to each one is given the manifestation of the Spirit for the common good. For to one is given the word of wisdom through the Spirit, and to another the word of knowledge according to the same Spirit; to another faith by the same Spirit, and to another gifts of healing by the one Spirit, and to another the effecting of miracles, and to another prophecy, and to another the distinguishing of spirits, to another various kinds of tongues, and to another the interpretation of tongues. But one and the same Spirit works all these things, distributing to each one individually just as He wills. For even as the body is one and yet has many members, and all the members of the body, though they are many, are one body, so also is Christ (1 Cor. 12:7-12).

There are endless possibilities for types of meetings when the whole body is involved. God has placed all of His creativity inside of Christ and this variety and creativity is expressed in and through His vessel, the church. People can share their Lord in so many different ways. Singing and speaking songs is only one of those ways. But let's explore another possible way that the saints can behold the Lord through singing and speaking.

Scenario #2

The church can create their own songbook. Now I realize that there are many wonderful songbooks out there already and they are filled with wonderful songs. But what I am referring to is a totally new and custom songbook for that particular group of believers. How about if the group plans some meetings where everyone will bring at least one song? This will be a song that has personally touched their lives and yet can be sung by a group. It should also be a song that is easily sung (I don't recommend you trying to tackle Handel's Messiah or anything like that!). Choose simple songs that everyone can sing.

Now what if you brought a song that you yourself actually wrote? What? Can this be? Is it possible? Absolutely. To tell you the truth anyone can write a song simply by taking a well-known song and then rewriting the words. How about taking a popular tune and rewriting the words to glorify Christ? Believe me when I say that anyone can do this. All you have to do is keep the same rhythm and rhyme. Let's take a look at a rewritten version of the song "Auld Lang Syne" that is usually sung on New Year's Eve.

I See My Savior in Each Face
(Tune: Auld Lang Syne)

I see my Savior in each face,
His love the tie that binds.
Our lives connected by His grace,
His Body, bread, and wine.

The grain is crushed: a brand new race,
His cleansing blood divine;
Our Lord revealed here in this place:
His life now yours and mine.

Our lives connected by His grace,
His Body, bread, and wine;
Our Lord revealed here in this place:
His life now yours and mine.

Your new songbook doesn't have to be made up of all new original songs, but different people can bring songs that have had a significance in their own lives and share them with the group. The only criteria I would make would be that the songs are definitely Christ-centered.

In this way, the group can create its own unique songbook that they themselves put together. And when you have the meeting to do this, the meeting itself can be a wonderful time of beholding, praising, and worshiping our incredibly wonderful and glorious Lord Jesus Christ!

"For where two or three have gathered together in My name, I am there in their midst" (Matt. 18:20).

Chapter Fifteen

Celebration

Some of you may be a little squeamish about the celebration aspect of being with the Lord together. This would mostly come out of fear from aspects of your religious upbringing or perhaps from abuses that you have witnessed among Christians. But please, *don't throw the baby out with the bath water*, as they say. This is actually a very beautiful and powerful way to express the Lord's life in you with your brothers and sisters. So please be open.

Dancing

> "...for this son of mine was dead and has come to life again; he was lost and has been found." And they began to celebrate. Now his older son was in the field, and when he came and approached the house, he heard music and dancing (Luke 15:24-25).

Miriam the prophetess, Aaron's sister, took the timbrel in her hand, and all the women went out after her with timbrels and with dancing. Miriam answered them, "Sing to the Lord, for He is highly exalted; The horse and his rider He has hurled into the sea" (Ex. 15:20-21)

...and David was dancing before the Lord with all his might, and David was wearing a linen ephod. So David and all the house of Israel were bringing up the ark of the Lord with shouting and the sound of the trumpet (2 Sam 6:14-15).

With a leap he stood upright and began to walk; and he entered the temple with them, walking and leaping and praising God (Acts 3:8).

Therefore, let us celebrate the feast, not with old leaven, nor with the leaven of malice and wickedness, but with the unleavened bread of sincerity and truth (1 Cor. 5:8).

Yes, we can dance before the Lord! Singing and dancing is a part of our celebration to the Lord.

Our Freedom in Christ

I feel that at this point in this book I should share a few things about the freedom we have in Christ. Here again, some Christians have thrown out the baby with the bathwater, mostly because of fear. The fear is that if we exercise our freedom then we will fall into sin. Of course, this is possible. However, we can fall into sin just as easily even if we don't exercise our freedom in Christ! And since when has fear ever been a good thing? I have known many believers who, out of fear, have not exercised their freedom in Christ. Because of this, they have deprived the body of Christ from seeing their unique expression of Him. (However, we should not use our freedom to offend another brother or sister's conscience.)

> ...that the creation itself also will be set free from its slavery to corruption into the freedom of the glory of the children of God (Rom. 8:21).

> I mean not your own conscience, but the other man's; for why is my freedom judged by another's conscience? (I Cor. 10:29).

> It was for freedom that Christ set us free; therefore keep standing firm and do not be subject again to a yoke of slavery (Gal. 5:1).

> For you were called to freedom, brethren; only do not turn your freedom into an opportunity for the flesh, but through love serve one another (Gal. 5:13).

In these verses Paul gives us a very complete viewpoint on freedom for the believer. First of all, the believer is now free in Christ. But what is the purpose of this freedom? He tells us in this glorious verse in Romans chapter eight: "...that the creation itself also will be set free from its slavery to corruption into the freedom of the glory of the children of God" (Rom. 8:21).

Wow! Do you realize what this is saying? First of all, Paul is telling us that the whole creation—that is, the physical creation (the universe)—is fallen because of the fall of Adam. When mankind fell, so did the whole creation. The beautiful natural beauty that you see around you is actually fallen. My wife and I live in a very beautiful place in Western Colorado. There are mountains, valleys, hills, trees, streams, and lakes everywhere. But all of this beauty is actually very ugly because of the fall of Man. The colors are dull and there is a shadow that lurks over everything. We can't see this shadow because we have never seen it in its former glory. But this creation is in slavery to corruption. I love to go on nature walks to behold the Lord in His creation. But sometimes I think about this fact that this creation is fallen. And yet, one day, this creation will be set free from the slavery to corruption into the freedom of the glory of the children of God! This is very exciting indeed.

Notice that the creation will finally enter into not just any freedom, but the actual freedom of God's people. Think of it. What kind of wonderful, glorious freedom this must be. Our freedom in Christ is so glorious that it will actually change the whole creation into a freedom and glory more powerful than when it was originally created!

And not only this but Paul tells us that this creation is eagerly awaiting (anxiously longing) for the revealing of the sons of God (Rom. 8:19). This is incredible. You see it's at that point, when the church is revealed in all her glory, that all of creation (the physical universe) will come into its own glory.

Other Ways to Behold the Lord Together

As a group, there are many other ways that you can behold and express your lives together in Christ. Really, there is no limit. Your imaginations are the only limit and that can be quite extensive. For example, let's just take the whole genre of the arts. I'm speaking of drama, painting, music, poetry, storytelling, literature, sculpture, dance, and so on. How many ways can you behold and express the Lord Jesus as a group through the arts? Let me share with you just a few examples.

Movie Night

I personally really like movies. Not all movies, of course. But there are many movies in which you can really see the Lord. I like to meet with a group of believers and watch a movie together with the express purpose of seeing (beholding) the Lord in that movie. There are basically two ways that we have done this.

1.) Invite saints over to watch a wholesome movie on a particular night. Someone will hold the controller for the television. When someone in the group sees something in the movie that reminds them of the Lord, they will say, "pause." The one holding the controller will pause the movie. Then, the one who called out "pause" will explain how they saw the Lord. At this point, any others who also saw the Lord can jump in and share their sightings as well.

2.) Invite saints over to watch a wholesome movie on a particular night. No one will hold the controller and the group will watch the whole movie from beginning to end. Then, after the movie, everyone will share their sightings of the Lord Jesus Christ and God's eternal purpose.

Of course, if you come up with other ways to do this go right ahead and give it a go. Experimentation is always a good thing. Sometimes the experiment will work...sometimes it won't. But you never know unless you try it. Remember, all of the creativity of our God resides inside of this awesome Bride.

*Some of the movies we have watched have been: The Matrix, The Notebook, any with a "Cinderella Story," The Greatest Showman, Avatar, Superman Returns, and The Lady in the Water.

Song Night

A song night is a gathering in which brothers and sisters bring new songs to share with one another. It can be any song that really speaks of the Lord to you. It can be a worship or praise song, a popular song (Christian or secular), or a well-known tune that everyone can relate to. Note: this gathering is not for the purpose of gathering together songs for a songbook. This is simply a gathering for spending time together in Christ using music. Of course, you all can still re-write popular tunes to glorify the Lord and perhaps put them in your corporate songbook. But the main point is just to have a wonderful fun time together sharing Him in music. Perhaps those who play a musical instrument can bring them and share a song they wrote or have learned. There are many possibilities here, and again, feel free to use your imaginations.

There are many other options using art. You could have an artwork night. At this gathering everyone could bring a work of art such as a painting, a sculpture, a mural, any kind of craft work, a photograph, and so on. You would bring this object because you beheld Christ in it and want to share that expression with your brothers and sisters. Sometimes it's a good idea just to hold it up and not share how you see Christ in the object. This gives the saints a chance to see the Lord without any outside input from you. You will be absolutely amazed at how differently the other believers will see the Lord than you did.

Storytelling Night

Have a gathering where one believer (or a small group) reads a story to the rest of the group. This can be out of a book or can be written by the saints themselves. (If you have a fireplace handy then that will help with the ambiance quite a bit.) After the story has been read, all the others can share their insights with the group. Some great authors that you can use are C.S. Lewis, Frank Peretti, Max Lucado, Hannah Hurnard, and John Bunyan.

I think you get the idea. Let the Lord within you use your God-given imagination to bring creativity into the gathering of the saints. This will not only inspire them to learn how to see Christ in new and different ways but also how to share Him in new ways with the body of Christ.

Beholding Christ in One Another

This is one of the most important aspects of beholding the Lord. Can you see Him in your brothers and sisters? How can you see Him? Let us count the ways. First, let's take a look at the gatherings of the saints and then we will look at seeing Christ in just one other believer.

Gatherings

There are many things you can do in meetings to encourage seeing Christ in one another. Here are just a few that have been experienced by believers that I know personally.

- Have a meeting where you honor just one saint (or a couple). Everyone will know ahead of time who this person is and will come prepared to share some things that will express how you see Christ in them. This material will come out of your own relationship and experiences with this person (or persons) or it can be out of the scripture itself (for this see my book *The Butterfly in You*) or both. Remember, this is not about saying nice things to this believer. It is about seeing Christ in them. There is a big difference. The center is always Christ.
- Have a meeting where the brothers honor the sisters, or the sisters honor the brothers. When I say "honor" I am not

referring to building them up in their flesh, but rather sharing how you see the expression of Christ Himself in them. These meetings will need some preparation. Each individual saint should come to the meeting prepared to share something. Again, this can be done in many creative ways such as through art, music, poetry, and storytelling.

- Have a party to celebrate the life of one particular member of the body of Christ. This will be a celebration of their life and how the Lord is working in and through them to edify the *ekklesia*. This will not be just a humanistic sharing of the person's life, but rather, it will be the saints sharing how they have seen Christ in that individual and what that has meant for the church.

- Do some *Jesus pranking*. Don't let the title scare you! These "pranks" are gentle and loving. You just come up with some kind of gift that reminds you of one of the saints. It could be a stuffed animal, a card, a candle, etc., that reminds you of that person in Christ. Put it in a bag, along with a card with encouraging words on it. Then take it to the residence where this saint lives. Oh, and don't forget to put a note on the bag saying, "You have just been Jesus pranked!" Put it on their porch, ring the doorbell and then run like crazy. They will never know who it was from.

- Place a card for every believer in the group with their name on it in a box or bowl. Someone in the group will pass the bowl around (keeping it high above their heads) and each saint will reach in and take one card. Of course, if you get yourself you will need to throw it back. Then, for the next one or two or three weeks (whatever the group decides), you pray for that person and then you give them a gift or token that expresses who they are in Christ (in their own unique way), or a word of encouragement, or some word that you feel the Lord has given to them. Now remember, this is a time of encouragement for the believers so keep it light and edifying. Have a meeting where everyone shares what the Lord gave them for that special person.

And the ideas go on and on. They are endless since we have an endless Lord. The purpose of this book is just to get you started.

Most Christians, if they have a devotional life, have it alone with the Lord. And yet it is within the gathering of the saints that the Lord is expressed and seen to the fullest. Just about everything you can do alone with the Lord can also be done with some brothers and sisters. Of course, you also need to have your alone time with Him as well. But it definitely should not stop there!

This every-member-functioning thing is crucial to God getting His eternal purpose fulfilled. The purpose is that the fullness of Christ would be expressed or manifested in all of creation (visible and invisible). God has ordained that this purpose only be fulfilled in and through His body, that is, the body of Christ. But for this to be fulfilled, Christ must be the all in all. In other words, Christ must be everything in all of His body parts. That's us! Is Christ your everything? Is Christ your all? Hopefully, this book helps you in that process of Christ becoming your all.

Final Note

The Need for an Experienced Organic Church Planter

As you learn to meet this way, you will also need the help of an experienced church planter. This person (or persons) will have much experience in organic church life. They will also have been trained by an older more experienced planter and will be called by the Lord to do this work. Please take note: I would not suggest that you try to establish a group on your own. You will need all the help you can get. I have been establishing and working with organic groups for the last thirty years. I have also trained several workers who are experienced in planting churches as described in this book. Please do not try and reinvent the wheel—you will waste lots of precious time. It's hard enough when you have the help of an experienced worker.

If you currently are part of a group or are considering starting an organic group like described in this book, I would definitely advise you to first read an ebook I wrote called The Organic Church. It will give you some good ideas on how to get some folks together, how to introduce them to some of the principles described in this book, and at what point to have an experienced worker (or church planter) come to help establish the group.

Here is a link to download the free ebook: http://www.therebuilders.org/organicbook.html

We are here to help you. Please don't hesitate to email us if you need help:

Milt Rodriguez: miltrodriguez9@gmail.com

References

The Life of Christ in the Early Church (audio) by Jon Zens www.searchingtogether.org/media/audio/ChristsLifeNoBible_JZ_Gainesville_FL_01-12.mp3

Jesus, Paul, and the Gospels by James D.G. Dunn

The Lost World of Scripture by John H. Walton/D. Brent Sandy

The One or the Many? The Pauline Vision & the Rest of the Reformation by John H. Yoder

The Untold Story of the New Testament by Frank Viola

Further Reading

A Short and Easy Method of Prayer by Jeanne Guyon

Searching Together by Jon Zens http://www.searchingtogether.org/media/audio/ChristsLifeNoBible_JZ_Gainesville_FL_01-12.mp3

Jesus, Paul, and the Gospels by James D.G. Dunn

The Lost World of Scripture by John H. Walton/D. Brent Sandy

The One or the Many? The Pauline Vision & the Rest of the Reformation by John H. Yoder

The Untold Story of the New Testament by Frank Viola

The Practice of the Presence of God by Brother Lawrence

The Community Life of God by Milt Rodriguez

New Day by Milt Rodriguez

The Butterfly in You by Milt Rodriguez

The Temple Within by Milt Rodriguez

Christ: The Sum of All Spiritual Things by Watchmen Nee

The Candlestick of All Gold by T. Austin-Sparks

Spiritual Sight by T. Austin-Sparks

The Torch of the Testimony by John W. Kennedy

The Pilgrim Church by E.H. Broadbent.

Movie List:

The Notebook
The Greatest Showman
Lady in the Water
Signs
Avatar
Superman Returns
Anything with a "Cinderella Story"
The Matrix

www.ingramcontent.com/pod-product-compliance
Lightning Source LLC
Chambersburg PA
CBHW051526150726
47997CB00001B/398